It is in acknowledging the small gifts received in our day-to-day existence that we are enabled to live a life of abundance. Russ Terry takes us through his year-long journey, demonstrating along the way how to experience joy simply by being grateful. He also challenges us to notice those things in our own lives that we sometimes take for granted and offers us new ways to look at challenging situations, including the massacre in CT. Russ's positive energy is infectious!! I for one am grateful that I have had the opportunity to learn from Russ's experience!—Kathleen Brady, career/life management coach, trainer and author of *Get A Job! 10 Steps to Career Success*

I'm a long-time believer in the power of gratitude. It's hard to be unhappy at the same time you are being grateful. In the extreme, if I was stuck in traffic, I would be thankful that I have a place to go; when my kids made a mess, I would be thankful that I have kids to make that mess. But one need not go to those extremes to benefit from the gratitude habit. For a practical approach, read Russ Terry's book. His warm and enthusiastic personality shines through, making for an extremely easy read. Along the way, as Russ awakens to the multitude of opportunities for gratitude, readers will learn to see the same in their lives.—David J. Singer, author of *Six Simple Rules for a Better Life*

D1473733

My
Gratitude
Journal

365 days of the people & things I'm grateful
for and the lessons you can learn from them

Russ Terry

iUniverse LLC
Bloomington

MY GRATITUDE JOURNAL
365 DAYS OF THE PEOPLE & THINGS I'M GRATEFUL FOR
AND THE LESSONS YOU CAN LEARN FROM THEM

iUniverse books may be ordered through booksellers or by contacting:

iUniverse LLC
1663 Liberty Drive
Bloomington, IN 47403
www.iuniverse.com
1-800-Authors (1-800-288-4677)

ISBN: 978-1-4917-2374-6 (sc)
ISBN: 978-1-4917-2375-3 (e)

Printed in the United States of America.

iUniverse rev. date: 02/27/2014

4.7.14

Jaime—
   Thank you <u>SO</u>
much for being at my
big Book Launch party
tonight. It really
means a lot to me
that you're here. I know
how crazy busy you
are.
   Hope you are as inspired
reading this as I was
writing it. Can't wait
to hear what you think!

Russ

FOREWORD

If I were responsible for coming up with the theme/title for this book, the first thing that would come to mind is the word "gratitude".

In this book Russ Terry does something that most men don't do too often which is swallow their pride and show gratitude for the amazing people and things that he experiences in his day to day life.

Not only that, Russ shows a part of himself in this book that I saw in him when we did our first interview, then our second, and then every encounter after that. He's found a light inside of him that is special and unique and is using it for greater good. He's made a choice to not cover it up and let it dwindle, but instead let it shine on others. Life can be hard for a man with society's high expectations for him to protect, provide and be a functioning member of society. Often times he's working so hard that he forgets to show gratitude for the job, the wife/partner, the kids and the friends that he's been blessed with. We sometimes move so fast that we often forget all of the wonderful experiences that we've had the day, week and month before, let alone see the value or find the time to write them down.

And take the time to write it down Russ did. He shows us in the simplest of ways to have a greater appreciation for our day-to-day life. It's not just about writing down what happened throughout your week, but rather detailing what you appreciated about *that* day in particular and sharing it. It's unfortunate that many people wait until Thanksgiving to express all that they're thankful for, and then never utter another ounce of gratitude for the other 364 days of the year.

It's gets you thinking to yourself, "Why don't I express my innermost thoughts and feelings on a daily basis".

As we go through our daily struggles, it helps to stay positive and to focus more on the good times than the bad and to find joy even in moments of sadness. I hope Russ plans to do an audio book, but if he doesn't, you can feel the positive energy and the appreciation for life just jumping off of the pages. You will be inspired, you will be uplifted and you will be grateful for the one and only life you've been given. I believe there is a book inside of everyone, and that book should express how *you* feel about life and all you've experienced in it.

For those of you who are trying to figure out your way in life this book will show you just how simple making a difference in the world can be. Be passionate about something, turn it into a useful product, share it with other people, build relationships and promote it as if your life depended on it. Russ's passion is clear in these written pages, he's passionate about life, has expressed it in the form of a book, he's sharing it with all of us, connecting with all of you and hopefully you will be motivated enough by his life stories to share it with others as you work on documenting your life's gratitude.

-Cheyenne Bostock
Founder, AskCheyB LLC
Best Selling Author of "Food, Sex And Peace Of Mind" *What A Woman Needs To Know To Keep A Man*

Acknowledgements

Thank you to all the people who gave me things to be grateful for during the course of writing this book. They are mentioned individually throughout these pages. Thank you also to my amazing editors—Barbara Hetzel, Kristin Knowles (who also doubles as my Publicist and did a very detailed review while she was almost nine months pregnant), Craig Washington and Byron Germany. The four of them provided many insights which made this book better. I want to say thanks too to my proof-reading team: my BFF Roxanne Jackson, who is a grammar guru like me, and my mentor, friend and colleague Dawn Doherty. Finally, thanks to my Mom, Diane Terry, for instilling gratitude in me even if I didn't realize it at the time. (Read the December 1, 2013 entry for one story of how she did it.)

DEDICATIONS

This book is dedicated to the memory of two people: my awesome Uncle—Augie Penecale—who became sick and passed away in the final weeks of my book-writing process, and Delores Lee, a woman who had a positive impact on every life she touched, including mine.

My Gratitude Journal is also dedicated to little Blythe Harper Knowles. Her Mom (my publicist, Kristin) spent hours and hours reading and editing this book in the last month of her pregnancy. Here's hoping being so close to gratitude right before she came out of the womb will make Blythe an extra grateful girl and woman as she grows up.

INTRODUCTION

Hi everyone! Thank you very much for buying my book. I appreciate you spending your hard-earned money on this. I hope in reading *My Gratitude Journal* that you'll be inspired to start thinking more about what you're grateful for. It's been eye-opening for me to see 365 days' worth of gratitude. I thought that it would be hard to come up with something new for an entire year. But guess what? It wasn't! Sure there were days when I hit "Ctrl F" in Word and found that I had already mentioned something. In those instances, I just thought "Ok, what else am I grateful for?" and, believe it or not, rather easily came up with something else. When you train the brain to become grateful for people, things and experiences, the pieces of gratitude keep flowing like a bountiful river.

I would love if people reading this book were to become inspired to start their own Gratitude Project—documenting what they're grateful for, every day for one year. My vision is to have a second book, which will be a collection of chapters—each from a different person who writes about how these 365 days of gratitude changed their life. Please let me know if you want to be a part of it! (I have given my contact information at the end of the book in the Epilogue.)

12/10/12—I'm glad I met Jacqueline Wales back in October and I'm grateful that I became aware of her excellent book *The Fearless Factor*. Her book, its message and Jacqueline herself are all inspiring. I had her on my Live Your Best Life radio show tonight and I got a lot of great feedback from listeners—they felt like she was talking directly to them. That's how powerful her book is. One of her messages is to write a gratitude journal. I've taken this idea and in turn, became motivated to write this book. I am grateful for this inspiration! I'm not sure what's in store for me over the course of the next year but I'm excited to find out. I can't wait to see how the book turns out—and what the feedback is— at the end of this journey. Throughout the book, I'm going to clearly articulate my lessons learned (so that you can easily see them and stop and think about them). Are you ready for the first lesson?

⇨ Lesson #1: Frequently think about (and perhaps document) what you're grateful for. As I learned in writing this book, it's an amazing process in so many ways.

12/11—For a few weeks, I'd been looking for some additional income to supplement what I make as a Life Coach, which isn't quite enough yet to live on. (I just started being self-employed less than nine months ago.) Today, two of my friends (Rosalind and Rudy) told me they'd like me to start working with them and their up-and-coming record company, Browns Town Music LLC ("Browns Town Music"). I'm excited, relieved (financially), and grateful for this opportunity and to them for thinking of me and putting a lot of faith and trust in me as they aim to take their company to the next level. It looks like it will be the perfect complement to my Life Coaching—an hour or two a day that I can do whenever and wherever I want. I swear—to paraphrase the book *The Alchemist*—if you put something "out there", the universe conspires to make it happen.

12/12—Tonight, I watched the 12/12/12 benefit concert for the people who lost their homes, etc. in Hurricane Sandy. It's heart-wrenching what some of these folks have had to go through. Hearing the personal stories of those who were adversely affected made me stop and be grateful for all the blessings that I have in life. When we become aware of tragedies, hardships, etc. faced by others, it puts our own lives into perspective.

⇨ Lesson #2: This is a common saying from a number of years ago but "don't sweat the small stuff". If you're fretting over something, stop and think if it's worth stressing over. If not, stop worrying. If it is, focus on what you can do to improve the situation.

During the hurricane, I was without electricity for five days but I'm glad I wasn't as negatively affected as some of these people were. I'm also appreciative that I had some close friends (Michele Marx, Anika Johnson and John Leonardo) who took turns that week hosting me in their warm, lit homes! As tough a situation as it was, it was actually quite wonderful spending quality time with these friends and their families over the course of that week. In normal circumstances, we wouldn't have been in each other's company for an extended period like that. I'm happy I got that extra time with them.

12/13—I'm grateful for my athletic ability. Tonight, I accepted my trophy for winning the Metropolitan Tennis Group's Summer Ladder, which had about 100 participants. I was basically a rookie—having played only a handful of matches the prior year—but I ended up the regular season champ and then after a round robin playoff loss to the 2010 champ/2011 runner-up, I battled back to beat my three other playoff opponents and then him in the Finals. Sports are fun and a great form of exercise—especially tennis. It's a sport you can play your entire life. As I write this, my Mom is 69 and her gentleman friend is a few years older. They both play a few times a week, which is likely a key factor in why they're healthy.

⇨ Lesson #3: Get out and exercise, regardless of your age or condition or "busy schedule". There's always something you can do.

12/14—There was a terrible school shooting today in Newtown, CT. Twenty children and six adults were killed. I'm grateful I didn't know anyone but it still doesn't make it any better. I hope that, by the time you're reading this book, the United States has enacted stricter gun laws to prevent more horrific occurrences like this.

12/15—Don't you love people who make your life better?? Tonight, my pal Parron Edwards did three great things for me. He treated me to a nice dinner (at my favorite restaurant) to celebrate the aforementioned tennis win. I happened to eat a big appetizer beforehand with a client, so combined with the big dinner, I was feeling a bit sick afterward and he got me some bottled water at the party we attended. It may seem minor, but it helped my nausea! Finally, he figured out what happened at the end of the night when the venue lost our coats. He is one of those awesome introverts. He notices what's going on around him while those of us who are extroverts are off being the life of the party. He saw that they took a huge stack of coats upstairs. He's a good one to have around—and I'm glad I know him.

12/16—I'm glad I discovered the website IndoorHoops.com. It organizes pickup basketball games in the NYC area. I've played in expensive leagues before, and this is much better than them. You pick when and where you play and it costs about $10. In the leagues, they tell you when and where you play and it costs about $20. It's an easy decision to me! I love my sports and basketball is the best one for me to play in the winter when it's too cold for outdoor activities!

At the end of each week, I'm going to ask you two questions. I hope this exercise inspires and motivates you to live your best life. I encourage you to write your answers, either on the lines below or in a journal or separate document.

What did you learn from this week's entries and what changes can you make to live your best life?

_____

_____

_____

_____

12/17—I'm grateful for having a radio show, for being a talented host, for all the smart, well-spoken panelists who have been guests this year, and for the 20,000 listeners I've had in the three months since I premiered. I'm having a blast doing it, and appreciate all the insight and positive feedback I receive as a result. I'm glad I've reached thousands of people with uplifting and empowering content (the words of one of my reviewers/fans—so kind of her). Tonight was my last show of the year. I'm thankful for this break from it for a few weeks (even though I love what I do, it is a lot of work to do it well).

⇨ Lesson #4: Be sure to take time away from certain projects so you don't burn out.

12/18—I love my clients. Today, I got the nicest Christmas card from one of them (Scott). He said "You're awesome. I know your business will flourish and you're going to be famous someday." Wow!! From his lips to God's ears! I always, always, always appreciate when someone has good things to say to me and/or about me. It feels good!

⇨ Lesson #5: If you have something nice to share with someone, say it. Chances are you'll make their day and improve their mood (even if they're like me and almost always in a good mood anyway).

12/19—I really enjoy being around my fun, giving and funny friends. They energize me! There's a saying "Energy attracts like energy" and that's definitely the case with my pal Ben Moon. He's the Asian version of me—a blast to be around. Tonight, he hosted an awesome holiday party/going-away dinner for a mutual friend. He cooked all day long—so devoted—and everyone had a really great time.

12/20—I'm grateful for my pal Rodney Lozier from the gym. He's one of the trainers there and because we're now friends he gives me free advice sometimes! You know how I met him? He was training his friend—doing abs—and I eavesdropped slightly and did the same exercises LOL. I have this saying—that I'm "politely assertive". That day I introduced myself to him and the rest as they say is history!

⇨ Lesson #6: Be politely assertive. It can help get you what you want—and some things you may not even yet know you want.

12/21—I got the best Christmas gift last night from my friend Parron. He bought me the book *This Business of Music Marketing and Promotion*. It's perfect for my new gig as Director of Marketing and Communications at Browns Town Music. I didn't even have it on my radar to buy a book. My new bosses were impressed that I have it. I can't wait to share some wisdom from it with them.

12/22—I had SO much fun at my friend Neel Gouviea's birthday party tonight. I got feedback from a few of the guests that they loved my humor and energy. I feel so great when that happens. At the risk of sounding not-so-modest, I'm grateful that others see me as funny, warm and charming—and handsome although none of the guests tonight mentioned that, but others have on other occasions LOL.

12/23—I ate lunch with a fellow Life Coach (Jen Kottler) today. Our conversation turned into an opportunity for her to be the coach and me to be the client. I felt much better after we spoke. Life coaching is an amazing thing—for both the coach and the client—and I'm grateful that it's in my life. In fact, it IS my life! It makes life much better.

What did you learn from this week's entries and what changes can you make to live your best life?

_____

_____

_____

_____

12/24—I'm so lucky that my sister April Terry Reavy shops for me. (She buys the gifts from me to her kids. I give her money and wrap them.) I must admit I'm not a fan of the extra activities at Christmas (shopping, wrapping, sending cards). I do love actually giving gifts though (and of course getting them too LOL). Anyway, she makes my life much easier. She's a busy Mom of two small kids and here she is making MY life easier. It should be the other way around! What a great sister and person she is.

12/25—Merry Christmas! This year, I'm grateful for the health of my immediate family and my friends. Everyone takes great care of themselves health-wise. Death is terrible and I'm glad that I haven't had to face it in recent years with anyone close to me.

On a separate note, I'm proud of myself that I had the courage—or presence of mind or whatever you want to call it—to not send Christmas cards this year. I know this may seem like an unusual thing to say, but the holiday season can be so busy and stressful and I'm glad I eliminated an activity that takes up a lot of time and was something I didn't enjoy deep-down. Instead, I sent a personal email to everyone who I'd normally mail a card to. This was much less stressful and time-consuming.

> ⇨ Lesson #7: Assess if you really need to 'do it all' over the holidays, and in life! Eliminating things is perfectly fine. The world won't end and your family and friends will still love you. I'm all about helping people live YOUR best life, not the best life that society or family/friends want for you.

12/26—I'm grateful for my niece Julia and nephew Sean. I got to spend a lot of time with them yesterday (on Christmas). They are the light of my life—SO cute and a joy to be around. Witnessing kids grow up is one of the best things in the world! I am fascinated by this process in general and them specifically. It's incredibly cool when each of them says something amazingly smart for their age. I think to myself "Oh my, how do they know that?" I also enjoy watching them grow emotionally. I left this morning and my sister told me that Sean said tonight at dinner "Can Uncle Russ come back so we can say goodbye to him?" ADORABLE!!

12/27—Tonight, I met up with Karen Collins and Jose Albino, two Life Coach friends who I am extra close to. I love the camaraderie, knowledge, support, motivation and inspiration of the other Life Coaches who I've met this year. It is an AMAZING field and everyone engages in COOPETITION—A Marie Forleo word for people working together and cooperating—not competing. (Marie Forleo is a popular Life Coach who has been interviewed by Oprah Winfrey and has her own YouTube channel.)

12/28—My friend Carrie Fiore Andrews hosted a Karaoke birthday party this evening. I had a blast! I really appreciate that she organized a great party (and paid for most of it)—fun venue, amazing people, great times. I sang countless songs and got lots of compliments, high-fives, etc. One friend of hers even said "you have a great voice" which was definitely the first time I heard that!! (I'm more of a Performer than a Singer LOL.)

12/29—I got a referral today from one of my excellent clients (Mari Ryan). I'm grateful to her for spreading the word about the great things she's experiencing as a result of our work together. The potential client and I spoke this afternoon. I think we had a great connection and I'm optimistic she'll want to become a client. (1/1/13 update—she did in fact become a client!)

⇨ Lesson #8: Referrals are excellent, whether for business or personal reasons or both. Think about how you can make a referral in your own life. For instance, many companies have employee referral bonus programs, so you can help someone you know get a job AND earn some money while doing it.

12/30—Last night, I went out for my friend John-Carlos Estrada's 26th birthday bash. Somehow the topic of age came up and his friends Christina and Doug could not believe my age. She's 26 too and she thought I was younger than her!! (As of this entry I'm 41!) The look on Doug's face when he found out my age was PRICELESS! This actually happens a lot (isn't that awesome—what an ego boost!). I am grateful I look young and give off a young vibe. Thanks, Mom and Dad for blessing me with great genes. That helps, but also I work hard to exercise five times a week and I maintain a healthy diet. I rarely eat fried foods and have plenty of fruits and vegetables and "good" carbs. I also drink plenty of water, which I've heard also helps.

⇨ Lesson #9: Eat right!

What did you learn from this week's entries and what changes can you make to live your best life?

_____

_____

_____

_____

12/31—Yesterday, I had a *Golden Girls* marathon with my close friends Joe Dudash, Luswin Cote and Charlie Hampton. Each of us is one of them. (We won't say who I am LOL.) Anyway, we watched eight episodes, which were hilarious. The best part though was the camaraderie, discussions, story-telling, laughter, etc. in the seven hour marathon. I'm grateful to have them as friends and for us to have the great connection we do.

1/1/13—I AM INCREDIBLY GRATEFUL FOR THE TREMENDOUS BLESSINGS THAT WERE BESTOWED ON ME IN 2012—I got cast on Wheel of Fortune—kicking butt in the audition and winning "five figures" on the show, including the trip of a lifetime (with my mom Diane by my side). I started a new amazing career as a Life Coach. I love helping people live their best life. Finally, late in the year I was offered and accepted a part-time role as Director of Marketing and Communications for Browns Town Music, an up-and-coming record company, which includes a free trip to Cannes, France! I can't wait to see what happens in 2013 (all of which will be documented here).

1/2—My pal Frankie Lugo and his girlfriend had me over for dinner tonight. That's one of the best things in life—when someone cooks you an AMAZING meal and you don't have to lift a finger! Just show up with a bottle of wine and WOW—delicious food that I have never had before. I'm still licking my lips. Yum! I'm grateful he invited me.

> ⇨ Lesson #10 comes from someone pretty wise—my Mom. As she always says "never turn down an invite—they may stop inviting you!" (I am sure I will have some other Mom-isms later in the book!)

1/3—Today is double lucky #13 (1/3/13) and I feel lucky to have two clients in particular—Mari Ryan and Kristen Foster. I had amazing sessions with both of them today. Seeing the progress in each of them the last few months has been incredible. I'm proud of them and happy for them. They also are consistent with having sessions every week, which I appreciate since I need to make a living at this new career. There's something to be said for being reliable. It's a trait I value and hold in high regard.

1/4—Today, I had a great call with someone who in part inspired me to write this book. David Singer, author of *6 Simple Rules for a Better Life*, spent about 40 minutes with me—sharing his experience, wisdom, specifics on self-publishing, etc. FREE ADVICE is another of the awesome things in life and I'm grateful he took time out of his busy schedule to help me become the successful writer that he is. He also agreed to write a paragraph recommending others read my book. YAY!

> ⇨ Lesson #11: Be open to others' advice. You don't have to always act on it but I've found that more often than not it's helpful!

You might be wondering how this fortuitous call with David Singer came about. I was introduced to David via a woman named Sharon that I met at a networking event. She heard me mention that I had a radio show. His book was newly out and he was looking for ways to promote it, which is why she connected us. David sent me his book for free and I am glad I read it. One of his six rules is to read a lot. Therefore, I set a goal to finish a book a month. The next book I read after his was the aforementioned *The Fearless Factor* by Jacqueline Wales, which inspired me to write the book you're reading now. Got all that? I highlight it because it's a great example of how something simple—going to a networking meeting and saying what I do—can lead to something huge—writing a book! Be yourself, say what you do and great stuff can happen!

1/5—Lately, including tonight, I've been hosting friends for dinner more often. The last three to come over—Dexter, Parron and John-Carlos—all offered to help. What a great gift that is! It seems simple but not everyone offers and having an extra set of hands to cut fresh veggies (which is the duty I gave ALL of them LOL) is much appreciated. I'm a bit afraid of knives/cutting—perhaps that can be included if I ever write a book on conquering my fears!

1/6—I'm grateful that being self-employed allows me to work whenever (and wherever) I want to. I'm leaving for vacation tomorrow and today I was able to have sessions with four clients—thereby earning money on a Sunday because that's what works for me.

What did you learn from this week's entries and what changes can you make to live your best life?

———————————————————————————

———————————————————————————

———————————————————————————

———————————————————————————

1/7—I'm grateful that my Dad remarried a lovely woman—my Stepmother, Marta. Not only is she easy to get along with, she's also helpful and has good wisdom to share. She's from Puerto Rico originally and every year we travel down there, which I very much look forward to! It's like paradise to me—great weather during the cold NYC winter, exploring San Juan and other parts of the island, incredible food made by her family or at local restaurants, etc. I discover so many new delectable treats and savor every bit of every meal. I love to travel so it's also nice leaving the continental U.S. and visiting the mountains and beaches down there.

> ⇨ Lesson #12: Spend time with people whose background is different from yours. You'll experience new things that will—as my Mom says—increase your awareness and broaden your horizons (Mom-ism #2).

1/8—I got an email today that I'm likely to be chosen to speak at a national conference for the fraternity Alpha Kappa Psi in New Orleans in August. I'm grateful for this opportunity—this would be my most high profile speaking engagement to date. I plan to give my "Live Your Best Life" workshop. It encourages people to focus on having a well-balanced life by resisting the pressure to work too much. In doing so, you can actually perform better at work.

1/9—I shot my YouTube series Weekly Webisode Wednesday from the beach today. In it I encouraged people to take vacations—because they're healthy, they reduce stress, they're fun, etc. One of my friends/Facebook followers (Kathleen West) thanked me and said that I've inspired her. Wow. I'm glad I've been blessed with this gift of inspiration.

> ⇨ Lesson #13: Think about what you are doing to inspire people.

1/10—I'm grateful for my step-grandparents—my stepmother Marta's Dad and stepmother. I didn't have much interaction with my own grandparents, other than my maternal grandmother or Nana, who had about 30 grandkids and died when I was 13. My other grandmother passed away when I was five and both of my grandfathers died before my parents even met. Anyway, Papi and Myrta are so good to me—driving me all around Puerto Rico when I'm there, making delicious meals for me, welcoming me into their home, etc.

1/11—Tomorrow, I'm interviewing my biggest name radio show guest so far—Paul Carrick Brunson. He starred on the OWN (Oprah

Winfrey Network) show *Lovetown USA* and has a best-selling book out called *It's Complicated*. Last night, he appeared on someone else's show and that host has great guests but could use a little grooming to be smoother on-air. I contacted him and he was very receptive and appreciative of my offer to help. We're speaking on Sunday. I'm grateful for him—my first potential Media Training client!

1/12—OH MY GOD! I interviewed Paul Carrick Brunson today and he shared SO much incredible advice—both for me as an up-and-coming Life Coach/media personality and for EVERYONE who heard or will hear this broadcast. Based on his relationship advice AND advice for life in general (work, etc.), I'm going to do some things differently to "up my game". I'm so glad my pal Chey B introduced us and that Paul said he now considers me a friend. The feeling is very mutual!

1/13—I recently got new upstairs neighbors—Dan and Drew. Since my building is a brownstone with six condo owners, it's rare for anyone new to move in. They did however and it's been great having guys like me around. We've hung out a few times in the building but tonight was the first time we went out together. I had so much fun and am grateful to know them. Running into them throughout the week enhances my experience in my home.

⇨ Lesson #14: Meet your new neighbors. Chances are they'll "welcome the welcome".

What did you learn from this week's entries and what changes can you make to live your best life?

_____

_____

_____

_____

1/14—Today, I posted on my work Facebook that I'd love for some people to review my book and give me feedback on what I have so far. Two friends—Barb Hetzel and Craig Washington—not only stepped up to do it but also gave me some great insights and recommended changes. They could have just said "it's great Russ" but they showed thought and courage and gave me some great constructive criticism. Even though I've known both of them for less than a year, I'm grateful to have met them and for their very helpful comments.

⇨ Lesson #15: Ask for feedback. It's likely to improve your performance, work product, etc.

1/15—Tonight, my friend Calvin invited me to see the performance of one of his co-workers from the Radio City Music Hall Christmas Spectacular. Yes she's one of the world-famous Rockettes! Anyway, she sings too and put on a great performance with her live band, which included her husband by the way. I LOVE 'live' music. It's so energizing. I appreciate Calvin inviting me. I'm so glad I got to experience it.

1/16—Today, the audience department from *The Wendy Williams Show* called me to see if I can attend tomorrow's taping. I'm grateful that a TV show calls ME to come! Usually it's the other way around! I guess I've 'arrived' LOL. Baller!!

1/17—The General Manager at my gym let me set up a table at the entrance today to try to get new Life Coaching clients. I thanked him profusely for opening up his business for my business. Three people are interested in my services.

1/18—I was driving around for about 20 minutes tonight trying to find a parking spot by 42nd Street in NYC—never an easy task. I was ALMOST late for my tennis match but finally found one about five minutes before it started. Parking in Manhattan is expensive and I was already paying a lot to play so I didn't want to part with another $20-$30 to park my car in a garage for two hours. I was so relieved for finding the spot just when I needed it. Simple things in life often make my day.

1/19—Last night after tennis, my friend (the aforementioned) Ben Moon and I had great one-on-one get-to-know-you-better time. Normally on a Friday night, as a single person, I want to be out mingling if you know what I mean OKAY? But he invited me back to his place after our match and I gladly obliged. We shared a bottle of wine and many stories. The most compelling of which was a story of his former softball teammate Eddie, who died in the terrorist attacks on 9/11. This guy was Ben's best friend on the Renegades and Ben had just spoken to him the night before. I'm now on the team and we wear a patch with his number (#5) on our uniforms. I never knew that much about him and am grateful to Ben because I now feel like I knew him too—he was a huge Yankees fan, loved to travel, and more. I probably would have gotten along great with him.

⇨ Lesson #16: Learn about those who passed away before you got a chance to know them. This can include not only 9/11 victims but grandparents, veterans and more. It's interesting finding out details on the person's life, and the storyteller usually beams with pride talking about the person they lost.

1/20—I was backing out of my driveway and didn't see a car coming in my blind spot. Luckily it beeped at me—helping us avoid an accident. I've never caused an accident in my 25 years of driving (although I've been hit a couple times). Thank goodness for this driver—someone I'll never know—who was very aware and prevented us from crashing.

⇨ Lesson #17: Drive carefully.

What did you learn from this week's entries and what changes can you make to live your best life?

_____

_____

_____

_____

1/21—I've recently made a new pal at the gym. Today was the first day we exercised together. Working out with a friend helps! It's motivating and helpful.

> ⇨ Lesson #18: Work out with a friend. I'm confident it'll make your workout more intense, which will in turn make you healthier. Also, having someone hold you accountable, in any aspect of life, is a VERY good thing.

1/22—Tonight, I went to an event at The Lubin House, which is the NYC presence of my graduate school alma mater (Syracuse University). I attended a lecture from fellow alum Walter Sabo. He's a top radio executive who was responsible for shock jock Howard Stern going from regular radio to Sirius Satellite radio. Anyway, I asked him about how I could get on the network. He asked where I was broadcasting currently. I told him Blog Talk Radio, where I—like the other hosts—am not paid. He actually said to stay put. He told me that my current platform—available for free on the Internet— will help me reach more listeners and Sirius doesn't pay that much to someone like me. I'm grateful for his advice. This is further reinforcement of the lesson #11 be open to others' advice. If it's being mentioned twice this early in the book it MUST be good so I'm going to take it a step further:

> ⇨ Lesson #19: SEEK others' advice! This is different from Lesson #15 (to seek others' feedback). From my standpoint, feedback is getting them to evaluate something you have done, while advice can be about the past but it can also be about something you should do in the future.

1/23—Today, my friend Jeannine DePaul Nelson, who I have known since 1985 (in other words, a REALLY long time) said to me via Facebook "Russ, I read everything you post every day and your positivity makes my day." Wow! Her saying that makes MY day! What a treat.

⇨ Lesson #20: Have a positive outlook on life. Doing so can help your overall mood. When you exude positivity, it becomes addicting and a great way to live. Furthermore, it can help others in ways you may not even realize.

1/24—I had some blood work done last week. I was a bit nervous about the results but today I found out that everything is fine! What a relief. Clean bills of health are the best bills!

1/25—I arrived in France. I'm grateful for this free trip (courtesy of the Browns Town Music team). The views in Nice and Cannes (both in the south of France) are spectacular. If you have the opportunity to go sometime, I highly recommend it.

⇨ Lesson #21: See the world! Until I got promoted into a global role in 2010, I had only been across the Atlantic Ocean once—for four days. Thanks to that position, I was able to travel extensively in Europe and Asia. Every trip was amazing and incredible. (By the way, my favorite city is Paris, followed by Singapore. Best food ever in my mind was a Belgian waffle in Brussels.)

1/26—We had a full day of meetings at the MIDEM music conference in Cannes (the reason for our trip). Our discussions are going very well and several business opportunities are developing. My bosses and I are excited about the potential collaborations that could happen as a result of our trip here.

1/27—This evening, I met Virginia Watson, the daughter of Johnny "Guitar" Watson, who was one of the most famous guitar players in US history. I told her about my book and she recommended that I add lines at the end of each week so people can summarize what they learned and how they're going to apply it in their own lives. I'm now doing that as you can see. I'm grateful to her for her idea and hope you love it as much as I do! Speaking of . . .

What did you learn from this week's entries and what changes can you make to live your best life?

_____

_____

_____

_____

1/28—We had an incredibly productive today. Wow. I set up a couple meetings with some high-powered people that became home runs! I wore some cuff links that were a 40th birthday present from my most longstanding friend—Kerri Blakey—and her husband Greg. (She and I have been BFFs since freshman year of high school.) Anyway, I'm grateful for these lucky cuff links and for her many years of unwavering support of me.

1/29—We had an amazing four days of meetings here in Cannes. Basically, this "side gig" of mine could become my full-time job! Can you believe it? We now have more trips planned—to Los Angeles for a couple things and to Austin, TX for the South by Southwest Music Festival. There are many potential business ventures as a result of our trip. One funny story: the new business associates we met there were impressed by the three of us and the robustness of the meeting schedule we put together (which was my job). They even went so far as to say "We need 'A Russ'". What a nice compliment!

1/30—I'm grateful I arrived safely from France and so far I haven't gotten sick! (Planes are full of germs as you probably know and the guy behind me on my red eye to Europe kept coughing!) Traveling wears down your immune system and makes you more susceptible to germs. I read a great article on how to reduce the possibility of it which brings me to my next lesson . . .

⇨ Lesson #22: When traveling, drink even more water than normal—you should drink a lot in general—and be tenacious about washing your hands before eating anything or touching your face, eyes, etc.

1/31—It was frigid in NYC tonight. I was at a book signing for my friend Cheyenne Bostick (also known as Ask Chey B) and met one of the artists on the Browns Town Music record label (Shot Dinero) and his lovely wife December. We had a great time, bonded AND they dropped me off at the train which I am VERY grateful for. (I did stop at Checkers and have 3 Cheeseburgers and an ice cream cone first LOL. I was starving—I hadn't eaten dinner and it was after 10pm! I'm so glad I have a high metabolism.)

2/1—Tonight, I went to my close friend Steve Gordon's going away party. (It was his last day working at his longtime employer.) He's the first friend I made when I moved to NYC in January, 2006. I always joke that he took me under his afro—he had a huge one before shaving it for his 30th birthday a couple years ago. Seriously, though, Steve helped me become the man I am today. Many of us gave speeches—including me and people laughed and nodded, which I always appreciate. I could feel the love and great energy in the room. I'm grateful for his friendship, mentoring, etc. He may be younger than me—by more than ten years—but I have learned a lot from him.

⇨ Lesson #23: Learning can happen from anyone. It doesn't have to be someone older.

2/2—I hosted a Taboo party tonight. It's a game that people can play at parties, etc. I'm a huge fan of it. If you're not familiar, your teammates have to guess the clue without you saying five taboo words. For example, if the clue is Bill Clinton, you wouldn't be able to say President, Hillary, Chelsea, Arkansas and saxophone or something like that. Anyway, I love the game and highly recommend it.

After hours of fun playing the game, it came down to a "Lightning Round" because we were tied after two rounds. I was the "giver" of the clues and my teammates and I got TEN in one round, which is the most I've ever witnessed in all my years of playing. I like to do things such as this—because they're fun but also because of my next lesson . . .

⇨ Lesson #24: Working the brain helps keep us from getting Alzheimer's disease. What puzzles or games, or other intellectual stimulation, are you taking part in periodically to make yourself think?

2/3—Today, I got an email from Greg Pilla—my most-longstanding client. (We've been working together for ten months as of this entry and likely will continue for a long time.) Anyway, after a great session, he sent me an email summarizing what he sees as his ideal February. (This is a Life Coaching exercise called Visioning—when you foresee something great in the future.) His email was so impressive and I think you can learn a lot from it. That's what I'm grateful for today.

Here are excerpts of it:

"I reached the position of Team Coordinator for my business two days before the end of the month. I went on a few dates. My productivity has been smoothed. A heightened state of productiveness has become natural to me. The painful disciplines have become routine. I'm waking up early and going to bed early. I enjoy making good food choices especially when I was out in difficult situations with limited options. My auto-responses to cheat with poor food options have been trained to recognize poor choices. My sister and I text regularly. I visit her without feeling stressed about work. I use my time with her to rejuvenate. My trip to Disney has been booked with my family and Trevor. I find time to grow new business with new people. I know this must be a focus. I meet new people. I build lists. I plan and execute. Plan and execute. I am an avid learner. I have lived in the zone—an alpha state. I respect my time. I sense each day. I count each day. I give people standing ovations with my actions. I live in moments, especially this moment. This was a great February, a big February."

Wow right??

What did you learn from this week's entries and what changes can you make to live your best life?

_____

_____

_____

_____

2/4—Today, I had lunch with my awesome friend Liz Rabii Cribbs. This year she and I will have been friends for 20 years! She's a busy executive with a hectic work and personal schedule (a husband, two kids, two houses to maintain and infinite kids' sports teams/activities) and she still makes time to see me every month. Over the years she's been so generous with her time and money. I'm grateful for her continued friendship. I am always extra appreciative of my friends who are mothers. I see how busy they are and I am thankful they carve out time to see me, text me and otherwise be an excellent friend.

2/5—Last night my roommate Jim told me he had an offer to move into a different apartment. Given where I am in my new Life Coaching business, I need someone in my second bedroom to help pay the mortgage. Would you believe that within one day I found a new potential roommate? This person is a close pal who I always share a lot of laughs with. I'm glad I mentioned it to him and he was prepared to move in. Problem solved almost immediately! (2/11 update: As it turned out, the place Jim was going to move into fell through, but at least I had an excellent backup plan.)

2/6—I applied for a well-paying corporate coaching assignment. I had to submit references to the firm to proceed to an interview. The following is what one of my clients said. I'm grateful and amazed at what she wrote. I include it not from a bragging place but so people can read it and possibly become inspired to be coached (if this story resonates).

In particular, what was it about the coach that brought value to the coaching relationship?

"It is Russ' way of connecting deeply with people, that created almost immediately in our coaching relationship an atmosphere of trust and intimacy and empathy that enabled me to reveal and uncover deep-rooted areas of challenge around which I needed to focus to create the kind of life that I want. Russ makes me feel like I confide in him—he makes me feel safe to share my fears and insecurities. He also brilliantly helps me to realize my strengths, recognize my achievements, set and accomplish goals, develop solutions to problems—what makes Russ stand out is that he helps me to see that I have all of the tools, resources, and faculties I need to create the life I want within me.

Since working with Russ over five months, I feel as if I am a brand new person—and I absolutely, unashamedly love my life. The "new" me lives an empowered life beyond my wildest dreams because of the life coaching I have experienced with Russ. Within every single 30 or 60 minute session with Russ, I feel as if a part of me (or old habit or limiting belief) is completely transformed. In working with him, I experience regularly what we dubbed "The 30 Minute Transformation", as in within 30 minutes of interaction with Russ—I feel totally altered in the most positive and healthy ways. I have ended every session feeling "wowed"—my satisfaction level with Russ' coaching is consistently beyond my highest expectation (and I am a tough, demanding, critical, client!). Through my work with Russ as a coach I've made bold changes, and incredibly improved: my career, my management of personal finances, my family relationships, my health and fitness, and more. It's been extremely rewarding to focus on one of the specific aforementioned areas, and then realize how the skills Russ teaches me are applicable across many facets of my life—Russ helps me to create this alignment and apply new skills to any area of life that I would like to change."

Thank you to said client for sharing her personal story and doing so in such an eloquent way!

2/7—Tonight, I facilitated my *Live Your Best Life* workshop at St. Anthony's High School in Jersey City, NJ (best known for a plethora of basketball championships under former coach Bobby Hurley). I love being around kids. They're always inspiring. Their mentors were there too, which was great to see.

I got some feedback after the session from a somewhat brash mentor who was in attendance. Even though she delivered the message in a confrontational way (LOL making a bee-line for me afterward and wagging her finger in my face—isn't that lovely??), I'm actually grateful for what she said and will incorporate it into future workshops, including one I'm doing in two days!

2/8—I'm relieved that I made it to Philadelphia safely today. There was a bad snowstorm (Nemo) in the northeast. See below for the lesson I learned! While I was home (I'm from Philly originally), I got to have a sleepover with my niece and nephew, who are beyond adorable. We played Wii and guess who won bowling?? That would be little three year old Sean, who got FIVE STRIKES IN A ROW! REALLY?!

⇨ Lesson #25: If you have to drive somewhere just before a snowstorm, leave early, before it starts! I wish I would have done that. This also applies to flights. If there's a blizzard coming where you live or to your destination, see if you can fly out sooner. Others may be trying to do the same but it's worth a shot.

2/9—My *Live Your Best Life* workshop in Philly today (for the Alpha Kappa Psi fraternity's regional conference) went AWESOME. There were 250 people in the room!! I'm grateful for the opportunity! I sensed that fraternities were a good place to tap into. I asked my friend Anika, who is involved in her local chapter at Montclair State University, if she could connect me with someone; she did—with her Regional Director (Naneen Christopher), who connected me with the fraternity's national office in Indianapolis. I applied for the gig and got accepted—all because of one request to a close friend.

⇨ Lesson #26: Don't be afraid to ask for things. Like the saying goes, it doesn't hurt to ask. What do you have to lose?

2/10—After driving back from Philly and sleeping only five hours, I traveled to LA today for my Browns Town Music job. We're having some post-Grammy award meetings this week. I didn't have tickets to the awards but was hoping to attend an after party or two. I even had my pal Parron design and make me a bow tie and pocket square for the occasion. I was all dressed up and . . . my bosses were really tired so we just stayed at the hotel. Hey, I can't have a great night every day. Not having success 365 days a year keeps me humble and grounded and for that, I'm grateful!

What did you learn from this week's entries and what changes can you make to live your best life?

_____

_____

_____

_____

2/11—We had an excellent meeting today in LA and, as a result, were invited to a show on Wednesday night featuring a pretty talented singer, who ALSO happens to be the nicest guy ever. His name is J Rome and he's the winner of the ABC show *Duets*, which aired in the summer of 2012. He's SO mannerly—holds doors, tells people to "go ahead" when he and you speak at the same time—just a true pleasure to meet. He deserves all the success that is hopefully right around the corner for him.

2/12—We had another excellent meeting today with the manager for a rather famous actor who appeared for many years in a prime time drama and is mostly a singer now. We're trying to collaborate with his manager on some things. His manager has many other projects going that would be incredible to work together on. I am thankful there are more possibilities of additional work.

2/13—Tonight, we got invited to the aforementioned J Rome's Valentine's Day eve show. Wow! He's an incredible singer and there were many other talented people who sang backup and/or were in his live band (which is the band of popular singer Bruno Mars). One 'backup' singer is a popular contestant from season two of *The Voice*— Jamar Rogers. Many people may recall his story—former crystal meth addict who's HIV positive as a result but has now been clean for seven years. He is an amazing spirit. These days, he performs AND is on the speaker circuit—inspiring others with his message of recovery and renewal. We hung out with both J and Jamar at the after party and they're both awesome individuals. Meeting them was so fun—and inspiring.

2/14—It's Valentine's Day! I'm grateful for having many things and people I love in my life. I may be single and while it would be nice to be in a relationship, I don't let that stop me from living my best life and loving life EVERY SINGLE DAY!

⇨ Lesson #27: Have a deep, intimate relationship with yourself. I promise that when you care deeply for yourself, have plenty of ME time and live a robust, balanced life, being "with someone" is no longer a necessity.

2/15—I'm glad I got enough sleep last night, which enabled me to work on the flight home from LA today. Usually I'm so tired I can't stay awake. I did get two quick naps in but I also wrote a lot of this book. I got behind in the last month or so and only had written the person or thing I was grateful for, and not the entire paragraph (and corresponding lesson, if applicable). I was able to catch up so I'm now relatively up to date. Writing a book is a HUGE undertaking— especially having 365 different entries. I'm glad I'm doing it and I'm going to work hard to not get behind like that again.

⇨ Lesson #28: If you decide to do a big project, set milestone goals for yourself and stick to them. Two different authors told me to set goals as it relates to my writing and I'm going to make darn sure I heed their advice. The process of goal-setting and achievement is an incredible, enriching experience—and one that will have a lasting impact on your life. The finished products we strive for will lead to incredible satisfaction, but the targets we hit along the way will also be rewarding.

2/16—I'm grateful I have AAA. After a long trip back from LA, we got to LaGuardia and first I couldn't find my car, which was like the *Seinfeld* episode except outside in the snow! When I finally located my car and went to start it, the battery was dead! This was at about 12:45AM after traveling all day—so not the ideal time to have car problems. Luckily I called AAA and someone came within about 15 minutes, which is pretty darn good for ANY time of day much less the middle of the night. I was SO relieved when I finally got home and got in my bed.

⇨ Lesson #29: If you have a car, get AAA. It's a great investment—only $45 or $50 a year—and gives you peace of mind in case something happens on the road (or in my case in a parking lot).

2/17—I traveled today to Montreal, Quebec, Canada. What lovely views driving through the Adirondack Mountains. They were snow covered, as was the terrain surrounding it, but the road was clear and I arrived at my destination without incident! I always appreciate seeing spectacular scenery and arriving safely.

What did you learn from this week's entries and what changes can you make to live your best life?

_____

_____

_____

_____

2/18—On my trip to Montreal so far, the guy I'm here to visit (Joachim) treated me so well—paying for everything—subway pass, Starbucks, drinks, dinner, parking, etc. I've experienced this "rolling out the red carpet" treatment other times in various ways. For instance, when I visit my dear friends Genevieve and Nancy and the Palermos in South Florida, they always have a ton of delicious gluten-free food for me. It's an excellent feeling to be treated like this. I'm so grateful for all of them.

⇨ Lesson #30: When someone visits you from out-of-town, treat them like royalty. Traveling is often exhausting, challenging, etc. and they'll appreciate you going the extra mile to make them feel special.

2/19—I'm glad I met Joachim last month. I had a great time with him the last few days. I'm looking forward to my next trip to Montreal or his next visit to NYC, whichever comes first!

2/20—I'm SO thankful I've gotten a good night sleep THREE NIGHTS IN A ROW! That NEVER happens to me. I can't believe it. I don't think I've slept that well in a year or so. Being self-employed is fun but since I've been on my own I haven't been sleeping as well. I think it's because my mind is always racing—thinking of ideas for my business—so when I partially wake up, the thoughts running through my head fully wake me up. Regardless, I'm glad for some much-needed rest. Perhaps Montreal is the best spot for it—Joachim's apartment is a lot quieter than mine and I didn't work much when I was there.

2/21—I'm very appreciative that Coaching is in my life and especially for my first Life Coach—the wonderful Linda Wassong. She helped me realize that 'personal admin stuff' was stressing me out, and the best way to reduce the stress was to handle it ASAP. I was tested recently by an issue with my driver's license. (I switched Insurances and also moved from NY to NJ and, for some reason, NY accused me of not having insurance. Both states were threatening to suspend my license—crazy right?? Don't they have anything better to do than accusing innocent people??) Anyway, I had to go through this long ordeal of faxing paperwork and going to the DMV. I waited there for two painful hours!! I usually strive to be judgment-free and positive but I must admit it seemed quite stupid. I share all this to say that "old Russ" wouldn't have resolved the issue quickly, yet would have been stressed out by it. I may not have handled it in time and maybe even gotten my license suspended. New Russ, though, was on top of it and, although it was challenging and tested my patience, I successfully cleared my innocent name.

⇨ Lesson #31: Stress is unhealthy and can take up to seven years off your life. Figure out what stresses you out and come up with a plan to reduce or eliminate it. (Also, never go to the DMV on an empty stomach! I felt like I was going to pass out!)

2/22—Tonight, I took one of those intense exercise classes at the gym—for free by the way—thanks to my aforementioned pal Rodney, who just got promoted to Assistant Fitness Manager and started this class as one of his ideas to drum up more revenue. I felt like I had to throw up, which normally is a terrible feeling (obviously) but I know it was an excellent workout and I'm grateful to him for inviting me.

⇨ Lesson #32: Do more cardio, especially if you are a man! My primary care physician says that weightlifting is just cosmetic and one should get the heart pumping fast at least three days a week.

2/23—This evening I saw one of my BFFs—I affectionately call him Frenchy. (He's from Paris and his name doesn't roll off the tongue so I came up with a nickname and it stuck.) Anyway, he's a close pal and client and has been very good to me over the years. It was great to see him and hang with him. We both live in Jersey City but because of our hectic travel schedules, we hadn't seen each other all year! I'm happy we got to spend quality time together and catch up.

⇨ Lesson #33: Make time for those you care about. Don't let "busy life" get in the way. Who are you due for a great catch-up session with??

2/24—I had a great day today seeing different friends in the city for brunch, shopping and basketball. After I played, I went to eat my favorite post-game meal (at Chipotle or "Le Chipot" as I call it to make it sound fancier). I was enjoying my meal by myself—which I'm totally fine with by the way. It's liberating and freeing actually. After all, I was with people all day and I don't mind dining alone—I just bring something to read. Magazines work best by the way (as opposed to books or something on your phone). Anyway, who walks in but two guys that I just met at basketball. I played on their team for a few games. They sat down with me and we got to know each other better. They're cool and funny and seemed to enjoy my company too, which I always appreciate. I'm surprised and glad that fate brought them to the same restaurant, which wasn't exactly around the corner and in NYC there are many places to go.

What did you learn from this week's entries and what changes can you make to live your best life?

_____

_____

_____

_____

2/25—I had an important interview today for the potentially lucrative Life Coaching engagement that I mentioned earlier this month. I'm grateful for the opportunity. However, one key point here that I want to share is my next lesson . . .

⇨ Lesson #34: Don't put all your eggs in one basket when it comes to job hunting. I see many people (myself included over the years) get excited about a potential new role or job and then if and when it doesn't happen they're disappointed. Keep pursuing other things!

2/26—I had the AMAZING Bernando LaPallo on my radio show last night. I'm glad I met his granddaughter Ekayani Chamberlain in December and she told me about and introduced me to him. He's 111 years old—soon to be 112—wrote a book at age 107, is writing another now, has never been sick a day in his life and has no wrinkles! He goes for a brisk walk every day, reads daily, and eats "food from the Earth"—i.e. no processed foods, but instead mostly fruits, vegetables, beans, etc. It was inspiring to hear his story and I got a lot of great feedback from those who tuned in. My friend Sheena even had her parents in Trinidad listening! Wow!

2/27—Today, I was telling my friend, mentor and fellow Life Coach Jenn Giordano about my book and she had an incredible idea: when I publish the book, ask people to take on their own "Gratitude Project"—in other words, they too would spend a year documenting something they're grateful for every day. Then, my next book would be a collection of stories from people summarizing what they learned and how they grew over the course of that year. I'm grateful to Jenn for all she does for me—support, advice and now this amazing idea.

> ⇨ Lesson #35: Make sure people know what you're working on. They may have ideas to make it even bigger and better!

2/28—This afternoon I got a lovely card from a client named Linda. Most people pay via PayPal, but she sends a check and goes a step further by sending me a card too! So thoughtful! What makes it even better is that she writes something nice in it. This month she said "I'm starting to feel better about myself and I'm glad. I'm enjoying time with friends and reading (the book I recommended for her) has been an eye opener. Thanks again for all your support". Thank YOU Linda for thanking me. It means a lot.

> ⇨ Lesson #36: Send someone a card with a hand-written note! It's a lost art and I bet it will really touch their heart.

3/1—I got selected for not one but TWO things last night!! One is the "held every two years" conference for the Alpla Kappa Psi business fraternity. This year it's going to be held in New Orleans, which is one of my favorite cities in the country. I've worked with them before—you may recall last month's entry about me speaking at their regional conference—and I'm looking forward to continuing to cultivate this relationship.

I'm also going to be a speaker at the 26th Annual Morehouse College Spring Symposium. The students are traveling from Atlanta to Alabama and will be visiting many of the spots at which the school's most famous alum—Dr. Martin Luther King Jr.—made history. I'm honored and humbled to be included! Reading the brochure gave me chills! To top it off, a week or two ago, I got an email that I had a free night at Marriott hotels and guess where the symposium is being held?! You guessed it! Marriott!! As I like to say, good things happen to good people (I must admit I often add "including me"). The school and its sponsors are paying for my flight and rental car. I'm excited about this opportunity.

3/2—Yesterday I had lunch with Luis Nunez, a fellow Life Coach who finished his training program soon after I finished mine. I'm grateful for and/or inspired by a few things as it relates to him:

1) He insisted on treating, which of course is a lovely experience for the recipient. He wanted my insight on some stuff and I was happy to oblige
2) Luis is from Peru and took me to a Peruvian restaurant. The food was incredibly delicious
3) He has an amazing, inspiring story. He wants to do a lot to help his country and would love to be the President of Peru someday! One particularly impressive thing he told me is that two days a week he takes a four hour bus ride each way from NYC to Boston to take classes at Harvard. His work ethic is incredible. Seeing him inspired not one or two but three lessons:

⇨ Lesson #37: Try different foods from different cultures.

⇨ Lesson #38: I'm all for work/life balance but, often in life, hard work is necessary to achieve one's dreams.

⇨ Lesson #39: Be around people who inspire you!

3/3—I had my pal Anthony Blackmon over for dinner tonight. I'm so glad we're friends. He's one of the smartest, funniest people I know, so it's just great having a conversation with him. We've known each other for about seven years and this was the first time we "broke bread together" one-on-one. Like me, he started a journey of self-discovery, self-improvement, self-awareness, etc. about a year and a half ago, so we had a deep discussion about all we've learned and how amazing it's been. We also watched an episode of *Super Soul Sunday* on OWN (my favorite show on my favorite channel). The guest in this broadcast was Marianne Williamson, who he didn't know of before. We were both engrossed in and enthralled by just about everything she was saying. (By the way, quick funny side note: I was so entrenched in our conversation that I burnt the sweet potato fries! Darn! The ones that weren't burnt were delicious though.)

What did you learn from this week's entries and what changes can you make to live your best life?

_____

_____

_____

_____

3/4—Someone paid for me to play tennis yesterday. I didn't ask, he just offered! Wow, twice this weekend, people paid for something for me. What a great feeling!

3/5—Last night, I went to the popular annual BNP Paribas Showdown tennis exhibition at Madison Square Garden. It was SO much fun. What a lovely experience. My friend/client/fellow radio show host Jenni Lewis works for BNP Paribas. I told her many months ago that this is my favorite sport and if she ever had a free ticket, I'd be very interested. Not only did she have a free ticket, but she got me into the VIP pre-party (where I saw my favorite player Rafael Nadal and also Serena Williams up close). There was also plenty of free food and drinks all night AND a suite to watch the action. I'm grateful for the entire experience. All of this was possible because of Lesson #6 (be politely assertive) and Lesson #26 (don't be afraid to ask for things).

3/6—I'm having a busy, exciting week so far. Last night I volunteered for an NYU FACES (Finding a Cure for Epilepsy and Seizures) fundraising gala. This cause is very close to my heart because my sister suffered for almost 20 years with this frustrating disorder. She would have seizures in school, playing sports . . . basically anywhere. Because of that, she wasn't allowed to drive and was dependent on my Mom and me to take her everywhere she needed to go. Finally, in November, 1996, she had brain surgery to try to cure her. It was incredibly scary. I'm inspired by her bravery—taking her life into her hands and trying to make it better. I'm happy to say she's been virtually seizure-free for the last 17 years and I'm grateful she not only survived the dangerous surgery, but that she's alive and thriving—married with two adorable children.

⇒ Lesson #40: Treasure your immediate family. As my mother says, "they're the only one you got".

My duties as volunteer at the FACES event were a "floater/runner". Therefore, I greeted guests and helped them with the bidding devices for the auction, among other things. I was on my feet for about five hours and was exhausted. I then thought about my Mom. She was a waitress for many years when we were growing up. I can't imagine how exhausted she was so many times—being on her feet for much longer than I was and doing it WHILE doing an incredible job raising two kids (on her own for a majority of time). I'm grateful to have such an excellent mother. She showed me exactly what a strong work ethic is, something I've carried with me in all my actions since then. She also taught me to be good with my money. I can remember my sister and me lying on her bed, counting her tip money for her while she 'unwound'. My mom often worked the breakfast shift which is why my next lesson is as follows:

⇨ Lesson #41: Always over-tip a breakfast server. They work just as hard as their lunch and dinner counterparts but the meals are often much less expensive.

Lastly, on a lighter note, the Master of Ceremonies for the event was new *Late Night* host and former *Saturday Night Live* Weekend Update Anchor Seth Meyers. He was hilarious and did an excellent job. I had a brief interaction with him when one of my tables volunteered to 'up their donation' to help raise more money in the live auction.

3/7—I had enough money to pay my mortgage today. I may not be rich these days from a cash standpoint, but I'm making enough to pay my bills without dipping into my savings and I'm INCREDIBLY RICH when it comes to life. I'm happy I enough money to 'get by' but also for this incredible journey I'm on—becoming an entrepreneur, building a growing business and best of all, getting paid to help people improve their lives. What I love most is being on the receiving end of their gratitude. I appreciate them for recognizing me as a catalyst and partner, putting them on the path to a higher level of happiness and joy.

3/8—I had four different things canceled today, for various reasons. Sometimes people are disappointed when they get canceled on but I look at the positive—that it allows me extra time to complete the many things on my "to-do" list. I'm grateful for this because I finally made some progress today on refinancing my condo. It's been something I've wanted to do (translation: it's been hanging over my head and stressing me out) for YEARS. I'm proud of myself for taking this step. I'm not 'done' yet but I at least found out my bank is willing to do it AND I filled out and sent in the necessary paperwork right away. If this goes through, and if I'm doing the math right, I should save "six figures" over the life of the mortgage, which is a lot of money!

⇨ Lesson #42: Look at cancellations as a sign that you were meant to do something else in that time period. Don't be mad at or upset by the person who cancelled.

3/9—I'm 25% done the book! After today, I've written three months' worth of entries. I'm proud of myself for being diligent with the process AND that I've come up with 42 lessons so far. I've successfully reached the first milestone goal I set for myself. It feels FANTASTIC!

3/10—Yesterday I saw a woman in my neighborhood who inspires me. I don't even know her name (which goes to show you that people can inspire others without even knowing it). This incredible lady only has one leg, yet I've often seen her in the gym working out. Wow. I'm grateful that I live near her and can witness her perseverance, attitude, etc. I think I may introduce myself to her next time I am in her presence. I want to know more about her.

⇨ Lesson #43: If you find yourself making excuses for not exercising, think of this woman who must use her crutches to walk a half mile to the gym, up and down stairs, from machine to machine, etc. If she can do it, you can do it!

What did you learn from this week's entries and what changes can you make to live your best life?

_____

_____

_____

_____

3/11—I went on a long car ride to Montreal yesterday and for the first time ever I purposely didn't listen to music. I just enjoyed the peace and quiet and tranquility of the peace and quiet. I'm ALWAYS around music and it's great but for some reason I wanted some serenity. I'm grateful that I had the idea. It was so relaxing and peaceful.

3/12—My ride home from Montreal today was uneventful. Thank God because last time, there was a lot of snow and it took me more than seven hours to drive home. I had a lovely time visiting Joachim. He's teaching me how to speak French! It feels good to work the brain and learn something new. In an ideal scenario, once I'm retired at some point in the distant future, I'd love to be fluent in four languages—English, Spanish, Italian and French. Right now, I only know some phrases and words in the last three.

3/13—I flew to Austin, TX today for the South by Southwest Music Festival (also known as SXSW—more on that in the ensuing days). I got to the airport and the plane had mechanical issues. Somehow I was booked on two flights, so, I was able to change from a layover in Houston which left at 7 a.m., to a nonstop flight that left at 9:30. It enabled me to have a delicious, relaxing sit-down breakfast—a bowl of all kinds of good things from a Mexican place. I received great service from the attendant at the airline counter and the waitress in the restaurant. For the former, I asked if I could email someone to comment on the job he did. For the latter, I gave her a nice big tip. I'm grateful for excellent customer service—it's a joy to experience.

⇒ Lesson #44: When you receive great service, spend a few minutes giving that person's boss or company the feedback. They made your day so why not make theirs?

3/14—While here in Austin we have VIP access to the Pandora "Discovery Den" at SXSW. They have a ton of performances by up-and-coming artists. When we were in Cannes in late January, we met (for about 10-15 minutes) with a Senior VP at Pandora, and when we told her then that we'd be here, she put us on the list! Hooray! It's so exciting being on "the list"! My favorite song these days is called Thrift Shop by Macklemore and Ryan Lewis. The two of them performed last night and were INCREDIBLE! We stood there for five hours to make sure we had a good spot. While there, guess who comes and stands right next to us but legendary music executive Lyor Cohen. He's a pioneer in the development of hip hop music and influential in the careers of so many artists, including Beastie Boys, LL Cool J, Run-D.M.C. and others. I was my usual politely assertive self and asked for a picture AND what advice he'd have for an up-and-coming record label like ours. He happily obliged.

3/15—Today, we had a couple business meetings at SXSW. Both people we met with offered to make connections for us that could be lucrative for our growing Browns Town Music business. I often did this when I worked in Human Resources and someone approached me about getting into a new group/department. The co-founders and I appreciate what these people offered to do today. They didn't have to. Karma can come back around, in a good way.

> ⇨ Lesson #45: Make professional connections for people. It's a nice gift to give and I bet someone will do the same for you in the future.

3/16—This weekend is my one year anniversary of being self-employed! I'm grateful to be on this journey AND to be successful at it. It was a big risk for me to leave corporate America and my comfortable life but I'm SO glad I did. I'm achieving levels of satisfaction, learning, happiness and joy that I didn't even know were possible. None of this was on my radar 365 days ago. I trusted that it was the right move even though I didn't have much evidence that things would work out.

> ⇨ Lesson #46: Trust your intuition, even if you don't know exactly what's going to happen.

I posted about my anniversary on Facebook, and got really nice comments from people, including the ones below. I'm inspired by what they said, and maybe you will be too:

Ayanna Lee—Boo, you were meant to do what you are doing. Everything you did before this was to prepare and give you the tools to be the best you are today. So proud of you! XOXO

Rosalind Conway—BFF, I am so proud of you. God will continue to bless you because your spirit and heart are in the right place.

3/17—This evening, I made dinner for the family I'm staying with in Austin. We had a lovely sit-down family dinner for six. It was an Italian feast. We had chicken parmesan and baked ziti and salad. I'm very proud of my cooking skills. EVERYONE had seconds and some people had THIRDS! (Even four hours later someone was saying

"Russell that dinner was SO good." Now, *that's* the sign of a delicious meal.) As we were sitting and eating and enjoying the food and each other's company, no one could remember the last time they "broke bread" together at the dining room table. It had been at least a few months. Needless to say, it was a lovely experience in many ways.

⇒ Lesson #47: Continue the great tradition that is Sunday dinner. Doing it with family is great but enjoying a group meal with friends can be just as wonderful (especially if you don't live near your family).

What did you learn from this week's entries and what changes can you make to live your best life?

_____

_____

_____

_____

3/18—I got an email yesterday from one of the people we met with while in Austin, TX. I sent him a note thanking him for meeting with us and for the names of people we should contact. I appreciate what he said—it made my day: "What I like about you guys is that you come prepared and that makes me want to work with you and help grow your business." Isn't that nice? He's helping us for free basically. I'm going to quote the old Boy Scout adage in the next lesson:

⇒ Lesson #48: Be prepared. Attend every meeting armed with an agenda and a short list of things you'd like to accomplish as a result of the meeting.

3/19—I received yet another inspiring email! Last night, I got a personal note from Lyor Cohen, the famous music industry executive I met last week. He clearly kept the business card I gave him in a crowded, loud bar, and sent such a nice email with all his contact info, including his cell phone number. I'm grateful for his note and his desire to stay in touch! Wow! Some people in his position would have deposited my card in the trash. Not Lyor.

⇨ Lesson #49: Whether you're someone struggling to find work or someone who is highly successful, a good old-fashioned follow up "nice to meet you" email is always appreciated and a classy way to conduct yourself.

3/20—I did my income taxes last night. I'm getting a good-sized refund. Hooray! As I've alluded to elsewhere in the book, as a new entrepreneur, money isn't coming in like it did when I worked in corporate America. I'm much happier though! That said, this will give me some breathing room to pay some bills before the due date and to take a couple domestic vacations later this year.

⇨ Lesson #50: If you anticipate receiving an income tax refund, do your taxes as soon as possible after you get your W2s and other forms, so that you can enjoy the extra money sooner rather than later.

3/21—Today, I was running late for my flight to Atlanta and then I found out it was delayed. I was so relieved. Sometimes it's nice to simply be lucky! I was able to relax, finish a few extra things at the apartment and leave things in better shape for my roommate.

⇨ Lesson #51: When something lucky happens to you, take a moment to stop, smile and enjoy it. The universe wants you to have some good fortune!

3/22—I presented today at the 26th annual Morehouse College Spring Symposium. As I mentioned earlier in the month, I'm honored to be selected for this school's prestigious event. My presentation was "Guiding You to Passionately Perform" and that I did! It was very well-received. I got a lot of thanks and positive feedback afterward, as did the event organizer on my behalf. It's always nice hearing good things said about you.

3/23—While I was down South, I was supposed to meet up with a couple friends. Both ended up not being in Atlanta at the last minute so I decided to stay at the Symposium an extra night. I had a great time playing my favorite card game—Spades—with some of the students. I was just saying to someone a few weeks ago that I missed Spades and needed to plan to play sometime soon. I'm so glad we played. I had a blast and it was a great bonding experience with the students, who were appreciative that I spent extra time with them.

3/24—I'm grateful for friends doing you a favor!! I have a radio show on Divorce tomorrow. As of today, I still didn't have a guest who was willing to talk about it 'live' on the air. Luckily my friend—the previously mentioned Carrie Fiore Andrews—agreed to come on when I asked her this morning.

⇨ Lesson #52: When a friend (or anyone really) asks you for a favor, strongly consider doing it. They wouldn't ask if they didn't need you, and it likely took some courage on their part to come to you.

What did you learn from this week's entries and what changes can you make to live your best life?

_____

_____

_____

_____

3/25—Today my laptop wouldn't turn on. Oh my God!! My book is on there, all my client notes, my bookkeeping for my business, etc. I'm indebted to the excellent technical support guy at the HP help desk. I'm also relieved it was still under warranty (by 17 days—talk about sneaking in by the skin of my teeth).

⇨ Lesson #53: Back up important stuff often!

⇨ Lesson #54: Don't try to watch TV shows online on random, odd sites you've never heard of. That's how this happened!

3/26—My radio show last night went so well. More people are tuning in, which I'm happy about. I hadn't had more "live" listeners than that in five months. Also, the content was incredible. Carrie and my other guest (divorce and mediation attorney Cari Rincker) shared a lot of excellent advice. I appreciate both of them imparting their wisdom. Divorce is a tricky area and I think the show will help people.

3/27—Last night, I met up with my friend Dana Mason. I'm proud to say that he's someone I'm mentoring. He comes to me for advice about his career but we also talk family stuff and dating too (not that I have all the answers). I'm grateful I have someone to mentor—it feels great to share wisdom. I always feel good after I meet with him.

⇨ Lesson #55: Mentor someone less experienced than you. This can be in any area (not just career but parenting, marriage, exercise, etc.).

3/28—Oh MY God I love LinkedIn so much. Last night I got not one but TWO emails on it from people who wanted to talk to me. One was someone I met once who had a business opportunity for me. The other person I'd never met but we have mutual connections and he was interested in my Life Coaching. I'm so glad LinkedIn exists.

⇨ Lesson #56: Use LinkedIn frequently. Even if you're not looking for a job it's an excellent tool. I know people who were happy in their careers but someone found them on LinkedIn and ended up offering them a job.

3/29—Today, I had a free session with the potential client from LinkedIn mentioned in yesterday's entry. He decided to become a paying client on the spot. I'm grateful every time someone chooses to work with me, but even more than usual today. I was looking at my income yesterday and my revenue was down 50% in March compared to January. I was a bit surprised by this but it just means I'll have to work even harder to make sure that I'm back on an upward trajectory.

3/30—My cell phone died today. It had been performing badly for MONTHS. I'd been meaning to buy a new one but hadn't yet gotten around to it. I'm lucky and fortunate that it stopped working on a day that was convenient for me—a rare "not-too-busy" day. I had time to go to my Provider, trouble-shoot the old one, figure out which new one to buy, and then spend a couple hours at home learning it, setting it up, etc. If this happened on a day that I was super busy I don't know what I would have done.

3/31—Today was Easter and I'm grateful that I got to see my Aunt Doll (among other family members). She's 81 now and will be 82 by the time you read this. She is still full of energy, spunk and humor and is a joy to be with. I'm glad she is still around and vibrant. Aunt Doll loves a good dirty joke LOL. I made sure I had a couple for her today. (I won't repeat them here—this is a family book!) She has a saying "I've got news for you" as in "let me tell you something". It's interesting because there's a song out now that I like by R&B singer (and Halle Berry ex-husband) Eric Benet called "News for you". He says the same line my beloved Aunt Doll says, which I think is pretty funny and cool.

What did you learn from this week's entries and what changes can you make to live your best life?

_____

_____

_____

_____

4/1—I got to spend some time with my Mom today before heading back from Philly to NYC. She retired right before Christmas at the age of 69. I'm grateful for her inspiration—she taught me how to work hard, which I still do to this day. Now I am inspired by all she's doing in retirement—volunteering for a local nonprofit, exercising more than ever, including tennis, Zumba and now yoga too.

4/2—Yesterday I had lunch with my Life Coach friend Filomena Iorio-Tasoluk. She had an AWESOME idea about me getting an agent! (As you may have gleaned by now, I am trying to do big things as a Life Coach, especially in media—i.e. on TV, etc.) I don't know why I hadn't thought of this before but I'm glad she did!

⇨ Lesson #57: Be open to others' ideas, which are similar to but different from advice, mentioned in a prior lesson. We can't do it all in life. People are smart. Why not use their wisdom to help us live our best life?

4/3—I played indoor basketball for free yesterday and indoor tennis for free today. Both are rare—especially in NYC. I've found that many places will let you try out their establishment. Yay for us! Why not do it, right? I am grateful for both of these venues and will consider joining in the future as my budget allows.

By the way, in basketball, I hit game-winning three pointers in two straight games yesterday! I was SO excited. I've never done that before. Although my shooting percentage may not have been excellent (it was still pretty good though), I'm not afraid to take those shots. I know basketball players who are hesitant—to shoot the ball in a key (or even non-key) situation. I also know people who are hesitant to "go for it" in life.

⇨ Lesson #58: Feel empowered to go for something! It can be big or small. Imagine the best thing that could happen (and not the worst that can happen). By going for it, you can achieve increased joy and happiness, maybe more than you could have ever imagined.

4/4—In the last couple days I've spoken to two of the Morehouse students who were at my presentation last month. They're looking for summer internships and I contacted five people I know in the fields they're interested in. EVERYONE wrote back to say they would be happy to help and to send the resumes along. WOW! I LOVE when people do nice things for others, without getting or expecting anything in return. The world could use more of it!

⇨ Lesson #59: Do something nice for someone—especially someone who can use your help.

4/5—In the last few weeks, I've had an idea to start a Life Coach Radio Network. I've hosted a show for six months and now want to 'spread my wings' and do something bigger. My vision is to have up to 20 fellow coaches and at least one show on every day. I ran the idea by a few friends (one of my mentors—Mark Schall—plus Anthony Blackmon and Dexter Cicero). All thought it was a great idea. Validation is an awesome feeling! Anyway, I posted about it on LinkedIn and Facebook. Without even casting a wide net I already have about 15 coaches who are interested! I'm SO excited. I think this could be something incredible and am grateful that many fellow coaches are enthusiastic about the idea.

⇨ Lesson #60: Dream big!

4/6—Today, I went bowling with many of the fellow Life Coaches I went through training with starting in March, 2012. That was a pivotal moment for me in my life and they were there from the start. They helped give me the confidence to start seeing clients right away, which I did. I've done a lot of great stuff since then and I'm ALWAYS grateful when one of them says how much they're inspired by what I have accomplished. One comment in particular blew me away. It's from my peer Graham Lowenthal: "You've set the bar really high for the rest of us". Wow! I didn't know I was doing that but I guess he's right. I'm thankful to him for what he said.

While I'm on the subject, I have to say this is the best group of peers I've ever been associated with. The knowledge sharing, intelligence, support, friendship and camaraderie are incredible. In looking back on my recent work history, I either was in a job without many peers or I had peers but to be blunt wasn't that impressed with them. I was being judgmental, which I am not proud of and have now been 'catching myself' when those thoughts come up. My point in all this is we all have much to learn from our peers, regardless of our work situation. I wish I would have been more open to my prior peers' knowledge. However, I can't change the past so I won't dwell on it. Instead, I learned a valuable lesson:

⇨ Lesson #61: Learn from your counterparts. They have a lot of knowledge. Also, who knows your employer, your role and you better than the people you're surrounded by?

4/7—I arrived in Miami this evening to visit my dear friend Gen Caruncho and her boyfriend Paul Simpson. Gen and I were reminiscing (as we ALWAYS do—God bless Paul for sitting through it and nodding like it isn't the fifth time he's heard some of these stories!) Anyway, she thanked me for something nice I did when I was her Human Resources Manager about four years ago. I always enjoy when this happens so I am going to make it:

⇨ Lesson #62: Thank someone for something—ESPECIALLY if it happened a while ago. At least for me, sometimes I forget the nice things I've done for others, and hearing that THEY remember, and that they're still grateful, is a really cool experience. It's pretty cool to have a positive impact on someone's life. I'm happy she reminded me of this story.

What did you learn from this week's entries and what changes can you make to live your best life?

_____

_____

_____

_____

4/8—Gen and I went kayaking today. It was her idea. I'm personally a bit afraid of anything where my feet are not on the ground. I've never gone skiing, snowboarding, a cruise, etc.—you get the idea. I was a little cautious but figured I should say yes. Oh my God I had so much fun! It was empowering to be there in the water and literally moving us around as I used every muscle to row from the back of the kayak. I'm glad that she suggested it—and that I did it without hesitation.

⇨ Lesson #63: Experience something new even if you're a bit fearful. You'll be glad you did.

4/9—Today, I had breakfast at Gen's, then went to see another of my BFFs—Nancy Alikakos Barbounis—and her family in Naples, FL for lunch. After that, I visited my "upstate NY parents" Bernie and Joe Palermo in Ft. Myers, FL for dinner and a sleepover. (When I worked as a TV Sports Anchor in Jamestown, NY, far away from my family, the Palermos were like my parents and I love them like they were my own.) Anyway, would you believe that all three of my hosts bought gluten free cookies for me?! Oh my God! Am I treated like a king or what? Having celiac disease—and not being able to eat gluten—can be challenging ESPECIALLY when traveling. I am grateful that all of my hosts today were incredibly considerate.

⇨ Lesson #64: When you host someone be thoughtful and ask if they have any dietary restrictions. You can even take it a step further by asking if they have any dietary preferences—i.e. things they don't like. For example, I CAN eat ricotta cheese, but man would I prefer not to LOL!

4/10—I can't believe I didn't mention this sooner in the book, but I have reached an agreement to be the Life Coach "on staff" for Blake Shephard Wellness Management, a group of Personal Trainers, Yoga and Pilates Instructors, Massage Therapists, etc. in the NYC area. I am excited by this joint venture, the cross-promotion between us and the additional clients we'll all get as a result (fingers crossed!) It's something that I've been working on for a couple months. The best part about it is that the company is doing some great new stuff (i.e. strategic partnerships and alliances) that could make this arrangement even more lucrative. (I got an email from my contact with them today which reminded me to finally write about it!)

4/11—Today in Sarasota, FL, I saw Nadine and Mark Macler, my friends from Villanova University, where I did my undergrad work. It was great being in their company and catching up with them. I am grateful for them beginning to motivate me to buy a second home in Florida. It isn't anything I want to do immediately, but it is something

I have thought about. I have many close friends down there (as evidenced by this week's entries). My job is "location independent" so I could spend a lot of time down there during the cold weather months. I look forward to working on this goal in the ensuing years.

4/12—I am happy that the young kid behind me on my flight from Miami to NYC finally stopped acting up. If anyone has a panacea for this situation, please let me know, so that I can tell the world! He wasn't a baby and the passengers around me were visibly frustrated by the disturbance (or maybe by the Dad, who wasn't doing anything). I'm not a parent so I definitely am NOT an expert in this area and pass NO judgment on parents. I'm also glad I got back safely. I did a lot of driving over the course of the week (visiting six Florida cities in five days) and am always relieved when I reach my final destination without incident. Lastly, I'm thankful for my friends, who hosted me in their immaculately-clean homes while I was there. When I walked in and saw how messy and not-so-clean my condo was, it made me appreciate the effort they put in to make their residence spotless before my arrival.

4/13—I love my work so much that I got home Friday night and that's what I did! "Old" Russ would have taken a power nap and gone out to the club. "New" Russ no longer needs to be "closing down the bars" as my Mom says (i.e. being there until closing time LOL). Coaching is awesome, and by talking about it here and in other forums, I hope I am inspiring others to, (spoiler alert) ignite the same passion in their careers and therefore their lives!

⇨ Lesson #65: Try to obtain a job and career that you love. Nothing beats waking up in the morning (or in this case getting home at night) and being excited about working. It's the best feeling in the world.

4/14—This morning, I went to a Christening for my BFF Roxanne Jackson's beautiful little daughter Sophia. I am grateful to God that he blessed Roxanne (and another close friend, Catherine) with their first children at age 40. We were all born in 1971. I always feel a special connection with people who are the same age as me. The similarities between these two women are worth mentioning. Their daughters' names are Sophia and Sophie, respectively. Roxanne and Catherine both gave birth to their first child at age 40 and seven months.

Anyway, at the christening, there were two especially touching moments that I am glad I witnessed. First, the priest recognized the organist. He's just 18 years old and making the music for a choir of singers two to four times his age. I am ALWAYS inspired when I am around talented youth who have the world at their fingertips, and in this case those ivory-tickling fingers could propel this young man to amazing things professionally.

The other cool thing was when the priest called all the Dads and their infants up on the altar. The choir sang *He's Got the Whole World in His Hands* as each father held his newborn up and introduced them to the congregation. I am getting chills all over again just writing about it. Many of us have experienced absent dads and the preacher wanted to remind ALL fathers—not just the ones up front—of their responsibility as parents.

⇨ Lesson #66 is to all the male readers out there. Before you have sex without some kind of protection (condom or birth control), make sure you're 100% ready to be a parent. If your woman gets pregnant and you keep the baby, whether you're ready or not, your #1 goal in life should be to be a great Dad.

What did you learn from this week's entries and what changes can you make to live your best life?

_____

_____

_____

_____

4/15—Today I had a session with a friend and fellow Life Coach. I am humbled, touched, proud, honored and appreciative that my peers want to pay me for my services. I think it shows a lot—specifically, that I'm at the top of my game.

⇨ Lesson #67: Are you so good at your career that your peers come to you for advice, guidance or even your services? If not, consider a career change into something that will better utilize your talents.

4/16—I found out today that the refinancing of my condo went through. I am incredibly relieved. I have wanted to do this for YEARS and ran into some stumbling blocks. Before, I was too busy with my old job to fill out the paperwork. Once I became self-employed, the banks wouldn't approve it because I didn't have enough earnings history as a solo practitioner. A new law was recently passed though allowing some people who couldn't previously refinance to do it. This will save me more than $100,000 over the course of the loan and will take eight years off my mortgage. Amazing right?

⇨ Lesson #68: If you own a home, refinancing at some point over the term of the mortgage is usually a good idea. In recent years, interest rates have been super low but they're now on the rise. Use your judgment and talk to those who are knowledgeable in this area.

4/17—I am grateful for the flexibility in my schedule that allows me to see friends often, especially these days when many people are so busy with family and work. In the last week, I have had Life Coaching sessions with FOUR friends—ALL women, ALL in their 30s and 40s. All of them are "going through something" right now—whether it's how to navigate the fork in their road, or deal with a challenging situation, or whatever. If I wasn't able to drive to them, to sit down and "break bread" with them or just see them, they may not have had someone to talk to about what's going on in their lives.

⇨ Lesson #69: Be aware of your friends. If you haven't heard from them in a while, contact them to make sure they're OK. When you see them, ask them how they're doing and use your intuition to delve deeper if necessary.

4/18—Last night, I got two nice compliments within about 30 minutes of each other. My friend and mentor Jeff Vilensky recommended that his friend—who is studying to become a Life Coach—meet me. In the email to his pal, Jeff said "Russ is a real go getter and a great coach—great guy to align with and work with." A bit later, I got a note from my main contact at a nonprofit center where I've given some free workshops. She introduced me to someone and in the note said "Russ has stood out and shined among those who have facilitated stuff here". I am appreciative of their feedback—both in giving it to me and sharing their feedback with someone else.

⇨ Lesson #70: Compliment someone. Be specific. We get performance reviews/feedback at work. Why not get them for the rest of our lives?

4/19—Today was my first softball game of the season. Now that the weather is nicer, you will probably start hearing a lot about my athletic exploits! I am on two softball teams and play in a rigorous summer tennis ladder. I also try to squeeze in basketball when I can. Anyway, I am excited for the start of the season. I love team sports and think they're great for many reasons.

⇨ Lesson #71: Be on a team (or committee). It can be great fun but also, and perhaps more importantly, it can help you strengthen valuable life skills such as getting along with others while also expanding your network.

4/20—Today, I visited my sister and her kids for my nephew's fourth birthday party. My schedule changed last minute, which allowed me to sleep over and bond with him and his big sister (and my little sister)! I am happy these precious children are in our lives. I know I mention them elsewhere in this book but I want to specifically say here that I am grateful that my sister and brother-in-law were able to adopt them—Julia from China in 2007 and Sean from South Korea in 2010. It's shocking that people would give up these incredible little people. (Anyone who is Facebook friends with me knows they're just the cutest things ever!) It's awesome being around them and being made to feel like I am their favorite uncle.

4/21—Today, Joachim arrived from Montreal for a visit (with his sister and her friend, who had never been to NYC before). It's great having him in my home for the first time. Also, I have been super busy and because he came down here instead of me going up there as planned, I was able to use the 13 hours that I otherwise would have spent driving up and back on work-related items instead.

What did you learn from this week's entries and what changes can you make to live your best life?

_____

_____

_____

_____

4/22—I made my French houseguests a traditional American breakfast of an omelet and pancakes. They were excited and ate every morsel of food. Afterward, Joachim's sister and her friend did the dishes. OMG this is the best thing EVER!

⇨ Lesson #72: When you're over at someone's house and they make you a delicious meal, offer to help clean up. They may be very particular and politely decline, but if they're like me, they'll GLADLY accept and will hustle to get you the dish detergent and sponge!

4/23—For the second time in the last week, someone described me as a "Go getter". I am very appreciative of this comment. I work very hard and it is nice that my efforts are being recognized, especially by people who don't know me too well. This feedback got me thinking about my old job. I was very good at it but no one called me a Go getter. It makes me think that, had I become aware of this back then, I may have explored a career switch sooner. What I am going to say is similar to the lesson from April 15th but somewhat different.

⇨ Lesson #73: Are you a Go getter? Are you super passionate about something (whether it's work or something in your personal life—or both)? If not, find your passion so you can live an optimal life instead of just "going through the motions".

4/24—I am excited that my Life Coach Radio Network idea has taken off in the last few weeks. I've had countless discussions with potential Coach Hosts, trained 10 of them already and have planned a big kickoff show for a week from tonight. There are about 25 people interested in being on the network, which has exceeded my lofty expectations. Moreover, they don't just want to be on, but they're excited about what we're building.

⇨ Lesson #74: Think creatively. What idea(s) do you have that people will resonate with and want to join you on?

4/25—Tonight, I was honored to appear on a panel discussion on career transition at an event hosted by my alma mater (Syracuse University). I had been looking forward to this for weeks. It's exciting to be "seen as an expert" by my alma mater, especially given that it's something that I didn't study while I was there. The audience was very engaged and was "live tweeting" some of the wisdom we shared. Among my gems that resonated with the crowd:

⇨ Lesson #75 (tweeted by TracyTilly): When you do what you love, the world can be an incredible place.

⇨ Lesson #76 (tweeted by SUinNYC): If you're considering leaving your company, go to a trusted mentor to help you decide what to do.

4/26—Today (Friday) through Sunday, I am teaching Life Coach Training for the school I graduated from (the Institute for Professional Excellence in Coaching or iPEC). This is an incredible opportunity—I am "in" the material for three full days, which enables me to sharpen my coaching skills. I am in the presence of an amazing lead instructor—my friend and colleague Cheryl Wilson, who is incredible to learn from. Finally, I am expanding my network to a broader group, establishing connections with the students that hopefully will be long-lasting.

⇨ Lesson #77: Look for opportunities to teach in your area of expertise. It's a great way to give back—and trust me it always feels great sharing knowledge and wisdom, and having people appreciate you for doing so.

4/27—At Life Coach Training today, one of the students said to me that they were talking the evening before and all agreed that they "loved Russ' energy". YAY! I am honored and flattered. I feel very fortunate that my natural style is enthusiastic and encouraging, fun and funny—and that this is resonating nicely with the group this weekend.

⇨ Lesson #78: As I mentioned back in December, energy attracts like energy. Spend time with people who enhance the quality of your life (and you theirs). It can be incredibly invigorating! On the flip side, feel empowered to spend less time with those who have negative energy or "bring you down", criticize, gossip, etc. Doing so doesn't make you a bad person.

4/28—I am going to be honest with you. I am striving to be a "judgment-free" person. I haven't always been this way and am still not where I want to be. In my small Life Coach Training class, there were types of people in the room that I have usually gravitated away from—a couple of smokers, a woman who's like the "Real Housewives", and the daughter of the CEO of my coaching school (and at my old job I had a big issue with nepotism). In the past I would have been like "Oh man, God is really stacking the deck against me" or something like that. But with each one of these people—and their classmates—I felt an AMAZING connection. I am glad I met every single one of them. I learned something from each person in the room. It just goes to show you that, when you're open, you can take a LOT away from any situation.

⇨ Lesson #79: Don't judge a book by its cover. Be open to having a great interaction with people who are not the type of person you may have liked in the past. It can open up some amazing things for you that you were previously not allowing yourself to experience.

What did you learn from this week's entries and what changes can you make to live your best life?

_____

_____

_____

_____

4/29—I just got confirmation from my 40th client! Wow! I got my first client last April and in a little more than a year, I have now had a positive impact on the lives of 40 people! I am grateful that my business continues to grow AND that so many people want to make changes in their life.

4/30—I got a touching email from a client today. We've been working together for eight months and she was in a bad work situation—17 hour workdays, a lack of appreciation and backbiting by her colleagues; there was no time for exercise or eating healthy, the list of woes extends on and on. Anyway, she decided recently that leaving this job of 14 years was the solution to the problem. It was understandably a very tough decision and something we discussed for a long, long time before she came to the conclusion that it was time to leave. Her last day was April 1 but she is no fool. Here is the email, which I am including in its entirety because it makes my eyes well up with tears every time I read it (and I have read it at least five times as of today's entry).

"I finally received my severance and I can now say I know what relief is. I worried they would find a way to not pay me, to hold it from me, to continue to ruin my life. But it is over now. They have no more hold on me and I am finally free. That is a sense of relief I have NEVER felt until now and I think this is the first time I have truly cried over this. I am in the best place I have been in longer than I can even remember—mentally, physically and spiritually. I would not be here without your support, your encouragement, your coaching and your friendship. You're changing lives, Russ . . . changing lives."

5/1—Tonight was the premiere broadcast of my Life Coach Radio Network! I went on the air for 90 minutes and interviewed 17 of the Coach Hosts who are going to be on our various programs. There was a ton of excitement among them and the listeners. I think we are building an amazing product that will help so many people—for free!! It will be interesting to document the growth of it in this book. I'm grateful a lot of my colleagues have 'signed up' to be on the network. I couldn't build it without them.

5/2—Today I got a note from Kathleen West, a friend and fellow Life Coach and one of the hosts on my network. I am glad that she's IN my network and ON my network. She had several nice things to say, which of course I am passing on to you!

"I want to give you kudos for last night's amazing program. The focus you gave each coach was touching. They were all inspirational in their own way. I found myself writing down the days and times for different shows I want to be sure to listen to.

Again . . . my friend, you have risen to another amazing height! Thank you for the opportunity that you have opened for all of us. Here's one for your gratitude journal: 'I am grateful tonight for Russ Terry giving me a platform to speak and be a part of such an amazing group of coaches in a new and amazing opportunity that will enhance my life in a HUGE way.'" Wow!

5/3—I have had two more prospective clients the last few days. Both contacted me! That's a great thing when you can stop "pounding the pavement" and work comes to you. There's a lesson in this though.

⇨ Lesson #80: Be tenacious in promoting yourself—that way when people need something in your field, you will be the first one they think of. That's how I got both of these leads.

5/4—I had an early flight to Los Angeles today. It's a Saturday and I had a birthday party to go to last night. I packed at 3am. I got maybe barely more than four hours sleep and had bad dreams about airport lateness and other mishaps. My dreams became a reality unfortunately. I thought the flight was at 9:06am and in the middle of the night realized it was at 8:06am. Things weren't lining up well to say the least. I left my apartment an hour and 8 minutes before takeoff. The NJ Turnpike on-ramp was closed. We had to go through neighborhoods to go back to the previous entrance. This made me late to the airport. At the ticket counter they told me that despite my 18,000 miles I lost my premium Silver status.

FINALLY, things turned around. Even though I was late and it was less than 45 minutes before takeoff, the clerk put my bags through and made sure they were at the front of the belt. The guy at security let me cut in front of others to save some time. A nice family ahead of me let me put my stuff on the belt before them. After I got through, I used my awesome athletic ability and ran like I did when I hit two inside-the-park homers at softball last year. I boarded my flight just as they announced "last call for . . ." I think I made it from my living room to my seat on the plane in 55 minutes.

⇨ Lesson #81: Do not try this at home! In all seriousness, arrive early to the airport. It will reduce your stress level significantly.

5/5—I am obsessed with having nice teeth and a nice smile. I had braces twice (the second time thanks to my great pal Darrell Willis, who bluntly and eloquently said "I think you need braces." LOL.) I floss every day and use a water pik twice a day. I never leave my home without brushing my teeth. I think there's something to be said for a nice and confident smile. Anyway, I am in Los Angeles and my floss ran out. (This is one product that is hard to know when it is almost done. Maybe I will invent a clear floss container so people know when to restock!!) Anyway, thank God there was extra floss in my toiletry travel bag. I loathe paying "hotel store prices" for anything. My lesson here isn't totally related to my experience this week but made me think of it. It's so long it needs its own paragraph!

⇨ Lesson #82: Keep a toothbrush, toothpaste, mouthwash and floss at your job. Many people brush their teeth when they first wake up in the morning and then have coffee, breakfast, lunch, a snack, more coffee, etc. By the end of the day, your breath does NOT smell good! I can't tell you how many times I've been to a happy hour or post-work event and was talking to someone with a halitosis issue. You don't want people to remember you for the bad smell coming out of your face but for the content of what you're saying and how you treated them. Depending on the time you have available, floss and brush, or just brush, or just rinse with mouthwash if you're in a hurry. OK I'll step down off my super smile soapbox now. Thanks for listening!! (Quick funny postscript—I was writing this entry on my flight back from Los Angeles and when I went to the bathroom after writing this paragraph I saw that I had all kinds of food in my teeth from my breakfast while waiting to board. Serves me right! LOL)

What did you learn from this week's entries and what changes can you make to live your best life?

_____

_____

_____

_____

5/6—I am in LA for a conference called MusExpo for my job with Browns Town Music. It featured a ton of panel discussions with many executives in the record industry. It was excellent hearing their advice and having a brief chance to interact with them. During one panel, I had the courage to ask a question in the Q&A. The moderator said "that's a good question". I am proud he and the panelists liked it. I consider this the utmost compliment. I hear it a lot from my clients, who of course are paying me to ask them good questions, which is the nature of Life Coaching.

⇨ Lesson #83: Ask good questions. We have two ears and one mouth and you can learn SO much in any aspect of life by asking others for their insight on something or to tell you about their life experiences (rather than going on and on about yourself). You might also be thinking, astute readers, that to ask good questions, you must be a good listener, which means being truly present in every encounter.

5/7—Today at MusExpo, music industry executive Daniel Glass received the International Music Person of the Year award. He was interviewed on stage by TV Host Jimmy Kimmel, who is hilarious and seems like a cool, chill, nice guy. Anyway, I'm glad I got to see their discussion. Daniel Glass is responsible for launching the careers of Billy Idol, Huey Lewis and the News, Wilson Phillips, Erykah Badu and more. He shared a ton of excellent insights, which of course I am passing on to you. This is perhaps my most robust lesson, so stay with me!

⇨ Lesson #84:

- Nurture others—he hired many people as interns who are now running the record industry
- Don't be insecure, paranoid, etc.
- Be progressive—don't hold on to the past
- Get involved in charitable endeavors—he is very involved with City of Hope Hospital in LA and also HIV and AIDS fund-raising
- Think globally
- Treasure your supportive family. He spoke often about how close he is to his wife and children.

5/8—Today not one but TWO of my awesome Life Coach peers (Karen and Marden) spoke to me about the concept of

Intention-setting, which is an amazing thing. I am grateful for their knowledge-sharing. It basically means that at the start of the day, you set intentions for what you want to accomplish, and you word them in a way like they already happened. Excited about this concept, this morning, my Browns Town Music boss and I identified the following as our intention for today: "We have come away from the last day of the MusExpo conference with multiple synchronization opportunities for our artists." (This means placements of our songs in movies, TV shows, commercials and video games.) By the end of the day, we met this intention and hopefully these opportunities will turn into a reality.

⇨ Lesson #85: Start your day by intention-setting. It's a powerful tool that can change your life.

5/9—The first 'solo host' to go on the air with her own show on the Life Coach Radio Network—Jen Kottler—had a great experience and sent me the following email. (I know I have been sharing a lot of these notes in recent entries. I will try not to do too many!)

"Thanks again for making this network happen. I really loved doing my show. Two of my friends called in and I had 30 people listening live! Also, I have had 64 archive listens! Woohoo! And I've listened to my episode . . . I did GOOD!!! Wow. And I had a blast! I LOVE THIS!!!!"

⇨ Lesson #86: Pull others along with you. It is somewhat similar to what Daniel Glass said the other day about nurturing others. The last time I got promoted at my old job, it was my old boss who created a position and 'pulled me up'. I had been trying to get promoted for a long time and I was grateful for him for his help to make it happen. In the case of my network, I like to think I've created a situation where other Life Coaches can expand their brand, get more exposure, help more people, sharpen their public speaking skills and have fun doing it.

5/10—I am grateful that I got back from my trip to LA without incident AND that I won't have to fly again for almost two months. I've been traveling a lot lately. Also, on both trips (out and back), I didn't have anyone in the seat next to me. It was lovely to spread out. I do have one lesson though. It didn't happen to me this time but has happened a lot.

> ⇨ Lesson #87: When flying, PLEASE be careful when putting your seat back. I can't tell you how many times I have been hit in the face, head, knee, computer screen, etc. when all of a sudden the person in front of me zooms their seat into the recline position. It's a combat zone!!

5/11—In the last week or so, I have begun to collaborate on three new and different work-related things. (I must be crazy, right? As if I need more to do! LOL.) Anyway, with one coaching colleague, I am offering a workshop to the public for the first time. With a non-Life Coach friend, we are using his certification as a Project Management Professional (and years of experience) to take people's Time Management to a completely new and higher level. Finally, a former boss who is also a mentor and friend hired me to be her part-time publicist. I am excited by all these ideas and collaboration opportunities. Like the old saying goes "two heads are better than one". Here's a little rhyme for you: I swear it feels great to collaborate! I really appreciate ALL of their ideas—many of which are different from mine. Working with them is helping me learn and grow, both of which I love to do.

> ⇨ Lesson #88: Consider opportunities to work on a project with people who are in your life. It can be business-related or a community service activity or anything really. (One caveat: working with friends has SOME element of risk. Note I said consider opportunities not rush right into something! I've experienced good things in these three cases but your results may or may not be similar.)

5/12—Today, I was home for Mothers' day and had quality fun time with my niece and nephew, who did great at the sports we played (wiffleball and lacrosse). I would love them just as much if they weren't into sports but I am happy and excited that they are. I'm sure you have figured out by now that I'm a sports junkie and being able to have this additional bond with them is neat and fun. I am proud of them for how well they did and can't wait for many more years and years of hitting, throwing and catching the ball in the yard with them.

What did you learn from this week's entries and what changes can you make to live your best life?

_____

_____

_____

_____

5/13—Someone close to me is being coached. I am grateful that she has taken that step and hope that it helps put her on a path to a more optimal life.

5/14—Today was mayoral and city council election day here in Jersey City, NJ (where I live). I am always inspired by the voting process. It's the great equalizer—people of all races, ages, socio-economic backgrounds, etc. come together to do something. Being in the building with all of them gives me that warm and fuzzy feeling. The woman who checked me in said "Wow you have such a big smile on your face." It's true. I LOVE the feeling of voting, the process, etc. and I am thankful that we live in a country where it's possible.

⇨ Lesson #89: The next time you vote, take in the environment. Enjoy the process, including noticing the others who are there voting, those who are working there, the voting device, etc. I promise it's a cool experience and a great time to 'stop and smell the figurative roses'.

5/15—Tonight, in a play that my friend and fellow Life Coach Cora Poage appeared in, one of the characters said "What do you want your legacy to be?" Isn't it funny how fiction—and a comedy no less—can inspire us? On my journey of writing this book I have been more active than I usually am in being introspective, etc.

⇨ Lesson #90: Think about what you want your legacy to be. It doesn't have to be career-oriented. It could be "being an excellent parent" or "helping today's youth through volunteer work".

5/16—I am grateful for people who are responsive, organized and just otherwise on top of things. Running this Life Coach Radio Network has me much busier than I already was. It's great and don't get me wrong—I love it and wouldn't have it any other way. Managing this network with the 25 of us is a big challenge (and one that I am up for). I'm appreciative of the hosts who make my life easier! I referenced this concept on Christmas Eve too (feel free to look back), so it's time this becomes a lesson.

⇨ Lesson #91: Make others' lives easier—whether it's your boss, a family member, a friend or even a stranger. It's a great way to give and is totally free! I bet they will treasure you for it.

5/17—I needed to do laundry badly today (for instance I didn't have ANY socks to wear to the gym) and luckily no one was using the washers in my building. I did five VERY FULL loads and no one bothered me. Sometimes gratitude is about the simpler things in life—like being able to clean one's clothes without being delayed.

5/18—I love when things happen as I envisioned them! Today was my debut on my weekend softball team. I am one of the two main pitchers and I've had to miss all of our games to this point due to teaching Life Coach Training and my trip to Los Angeles. We were 0-5 before I took the mound today. In the days leading up to this, I took part in the art of Visioning—i.e. picturing what it would be like when something desirable happens in the future. I imagined leading my team to victory with a great pitching effort and my teammates being appreciative of my performance. That's exactly what transpired. I gave up just two unearned runs against a previously-unbeaten team and we finally got our first win of the year!

⇨ Lesson #92: What can you Vision for yourself? If you think about the specifics of what your dream(s) would be like, then the chances of it/them coming true are exponentially higher!

5/19—Today was my first official appearance as a part of Blake Shephard Wellness Management. We were the official warmer-uppers of the crowd at the NYC AIDS Walk. It was cool being on stage (bright and early) before the celebrities and having the people in the audience cheer for us. After we were done, I stayed to watch all the speeches in the opening ceremony. The most moving one was from a woman who's living with HIV. She had never done ANY public speaking before and what she said and more importantly how she said it was moving. Some of the celebs were reading from a script. This woman wasn't. She spoke from the heart and told her story. I had tears running down my face.

⇨ Lesson #93: When you're speaking in front of a crowd—big or small—be passionate, real and conversational. Chances are no one will know if you didn't say exactly what you intended to.

What did you learn from this week's entries and what changes can you make to live your best life?

_____

_____

_____

_____

5/20—Last night I had dinner with my friend Jay Moore. He mentioned something called a birthday epiphany. Every year on the anniversary of the day he was born, he reflects on his current life status and thinks hard about what "changes-for-the-good" he can make to live a more optimal life. I love this idea! What a great way to check in with yourself.

⇨ Lesson #94: What's your birthday epiphany going to be this year?

5/21—I took my friend Jenni Lewis out to lunch today. My growing media empire is happening because of her and I wanted to express my gratitude to her and for her. In the summer of 2012, she had me on a segment of her radio show. She liked it so much, she had me back for a full hour, then another full hour, and then when she started her own network, she made me the first host on it. This all happened within two months. I am glad she saw my talent and potential and that she gave me the platform to showcase it. I owe it all to her!

5/22—Tonight, I went over to my dear friend Liz Rabii Cribbs' house for dinner. It's always a wonderful time catching up with her and seeing her family. During my visit I was impressed to see that her daughter Cassie is doing some fundraising. It's cool that this seven year old already has "making the world a better place" on her radar. I was honored to be asked to donate and gladly handed over some money.

⇨ Lesson #95: If you're a parent, teach your kids the benefits of fundraising at an early age. You'll set them up to leave a great legacy on the world.

5/23—Today, I took part in some free training offered to new Blog Talk Radio stations. (Even though our network has been on for a few weeks I hadn't yet had the chance to participate.) I learned a few things and am always glad when that happens. Best of all, many trainings (including this one) are free.

⇨ Lesson #96: If your job or a project you're involved with offers you the chance to learn more, take it! Many employers have in-house training, graduate school tuition reimbursement, etc.

5/24—I had three absent-minded things happen in the last few days. I left my glove at Central Park after my softball game. I bought movie tickets for the wrong day. I forgot my groceries at the store. I'm actually happy that these happened in close proximity to each other. It led me to reflect and be coached in this area. As a result of a great discussion with my awesome Life Coach Radio Network colleague and now friend Danielle Mercurio, she helped me realize a few things:

1) I'm busy and things ARE going to fall through the cracks
2) I am going to 'go easy on myself' when they do
3) I am going to 'be more present' in whatever I'm doing, which will hopefully help me to be less forgetful.

Coaching is great! I love this stuff.

5/25—I always say music is the soundtrack to our lives. I love that it evokes memories, is a reminder to contact someone (when you hear a song that reminds you of them), and that it makes me smile or tap my foot or just SING OUT LOUD! Tonight, I went to a karaoke birthday party for my awesome wing man Craig Washington. It was incredibly fun. I sang a ton of songs and the other guests loved my performances. I feel at home in front of an audience, especially one that seems to be enjoying my talents.

5/26—I love the randomness of life. Today I was texting with my original BFF—Nancy Alikakos Barbounis. I'm always appreciative when she has time to chat with me. She's a busy Mom of two young boys. When I rejoined my now former employer (PwC) in December, 2005, she was in the cube to the left of me. Had we not been seated next to each other, maybe we wouldn't have developed the incredible bond we still have to this day. She is one of the funniest people I know. She's also so smart, so seasoned—or "4-S" as I used to tell her. Nancy also has the most amazing memory! Her sister Maria Alikakos and I always joke that it's like a steel trap. Nancy remembers WAY more about me than even I do! I'm grateful for that and her friendship and her always making me laugh out loud. Thank you, cubicle Gods for putting us next to each other!

What did you learn from this week's entries and what changes can you make to live your best life?

_____

_____

_____

_____

5/27—I am thankful for the soldiers that fight for us and also for their families, who are strong despite their loved ones being at risk. Today is Memorial Day and I am amazed at the courage of these men and women who put their lives on the line to protect our country.

⇨ Lesson #97: Think about what you can do for our military personnel or their families. Can you hire someone who is back from overseas? Say a prayer for the people in a war zone and their loved ones who are separated from them?

5/28—I'm grateful for Facebook! First of all, it's fun. It's great interacting with friends from all over who I don't see regularly. Secondly, it's an EXCELLENT way to market my business. Everyone in my circle knows I'm a Life Coach and I appreciate that it's helping me to make a living! Thirdly, the mutual friends feature is amazing. I made a new pal at the AIDS Walk recently (Daniel Magyar-Cloudt) and we realized that we have a close friend (Billy Sanders, who lives in London) in common. If it wasn't for Facebook, I can't imagine we ever would have figured that out. Knowing this made our new bond even stronger. It also gave me a reason to catch up with Billy!

5/29—I got this note yesterday from a fan of my Life Coach Radio Network: "I'm an avid listener to your radio shows. Thank you SO MUCH for putting it together :) Please keep up the great work—your shows ROCK! What you're doing is great and I know that anyone that listens with an open heart and mind can benefit greatly from your work." Wow! This was so nice of him. Even though we're still in the first month, I'm happy that what we're doing is resonating with people and they are enjoying it.

5/30—You won't believe this, but my lost softball glove has been found! Who would think that something lost in NYC's Central Park would make its way back to its owner?! YAY! Today was our next game, after the game that I lost it. I was looking around for it (a week later, LOL) and my smart teammate Rob said "Why don't you ask them (the team that preceded us on this bench area) if they've seen it?" As it turns out, they played after us last week. The captain noticed my glove was left behind and took it with him. We exchanged info and made a plan for me to go to his office to get it.

⇨ Lesson #98: If you can help someone out who lost something, please do it! They'll appreciate it!

5/31—Last night I took the Myers-Briggs personality assessment. It's always cool doing things such as this. It reminds me of a similar exercise called What Color Are You (or something like that) that I did at least five years ago. It indicated to me that my work style was a certain way. It also helped me realize that two colleagues who I was collaborating with on a project were a different 'color'. Learning how best to interact with them based on their personality helped the three of us turn the project from not-so-great into much better. I don't know who said the next quote but it's a good one and relevant here.

⇨ Lesson #99: Instead of treating others like YOU would like to be treated, treat them how THEY want to be treated. There's often a difference!

6/1—I kept meaning to write about this earlier this year and never did so I'm writing about it today. I'm grateful for my sense of humor. My record label bosses so often laugh at the funny things I say. They even plead with me sometimes "please Russell stop I'm tired from laughing so much" LOL. It's great being around people who appreciate me—whether it's for my humor, my work ethic, my people skills or all of the above.

⇨ Lesson #100: Surround yourself with people who value and appreciate you!

⇨ Lesson #101: Laugh as much as you can. It feels good and is healthy.

6/2—Last night, I was at my friend Bryan Barrett's cookout and met his friend and mentor Jimi. More than a year and a half ago, I saw an annual performance they put on. It was kind of like a local version of Cirque de Soleil meets fashion show meets dancing. I had a great time that evening. Apparently, so much so that as soon as I arrived at the BBQ, Jimi came up to me and said "Oh my God, you're Bryan's friend Russ! We LOVED your enthusiasm when we saw the video of our 2011 show! You were right there in front of the stage. It was great seeing you enjoy our performances so much. THANK YOU!!!!" Wow I was stunned! I had NO idea that being in the audience can make the performers and organizers happy.

⇨ Lesson #102: If you love a play, musical, concert or any other artistic endeavor, show your joy and support with unbridled enthusiasm.

What did you learn from this week's entries and what changes can you make to live your best life?

_____

_____

_____

_____

6/3—Almost every Monday night for the last month or two, I have attended an amazing thing called Soul Night at Toshi's, organized by my new friend—the super-talented Shira Elias. She brings together some AMAZING up-and-coming singers to perform classic songs by Marvin Gaye, Michael Jackson, Jill Scott and many more. It's quickly become the highlight of my week and a can't-miss thing. The musicians (live band and singers) have a great gift and I'm glad I experience it every week. I often go by myself (which, by the way, is very empowering.) Becoming your own best friend is the single most gratifying relationship you can have.

⇨ Lesson #103: Enjoy experiences such as dinner, movies, going out and traveling on your own. I bet you'll live life in a great new way.

On this night, I went there solo and sat at a table by myself. Before I knew it, two of my FAVORITE singers came and sat with ME! Wow! I had met them briefly a few times and told them I was a fan of their work. I was excited to experience the night in a new way, side-by-side with greatness. I am grateful that Angela Birchett and Jared Joseph graced me with their presence tonight. Don't forget their names. I firmly believe they're going to be STARS! They already are in my eyes.

6/4—I love that chill/shiver you get when you experience something amazing. I was watching *The Voice* tonight. One of the performers (the eventual second place finisher—Michelle Chamuel) ALWAYS gives me this feeling. She exudes such incredible passion, evoking in me that face-tingling, blood rushing upward, shoulders shivering moment. I've enjoyed watching her grow this season, AND seeing her develop an amazing bond with one of my favorite musicians—Usher, who is her coach on the show. It's been cool seeing him in a new light and I'm excited that he and Shakira are scheduled to return to the show in spring 2014.

6/5—I found out today that the Life Coach Radio Network is now "featured" on Blog Talk Radio. YAY! This means that BTR will now start promoting us (in addition to us promoting ourselves). If you build it, they will come.

⇨ Lesson #104: What are YOU building? It doesn't have to be something career-related. It could be a loving and supportive family, a nonprofit endeavor, etc.

6/6—I finally got my softball glove back today. The guy who found it shared a great idea with me. It's simple but can save a lot of hassle and heart ache if you think about it:

⇨ Lesson #105: Put your name and phone number on key possessions. This will make it much easier if/when you lose them!

6/7—Last night, I had a tennis match and it literally started raining as soon as I arrived at the park! Ugh! However, after about 15 minutes of hard rain, it let up enough for us to play for at least an hour. I was really looking forward to facing this tough opponent and I am glad I got to do so and also get some exercise in.

6/8—I just joined Instagram. It has a cool feature that allows you to instantly follow all your Facebook friends who are on it. So cool and convenient—and beneficial for an entrepreneur! You then get notifications when someone follows you back. I saw that someone I met and taught once in a 90 minute workshop about seven months ago—Christina Dechert—followed me and has a quote from MY session as her profile sentence:

"Rather than being your own worst enemy, how about instead being your OWN BEST FRIEND?"

I am honored! It's actually my inspiration for this book—Jacqueline Wales—who says that in her book *The Fearless Factor*. I contacted Christine to say how touched and honored I was that she has the quote in her profile. She wrote back and said "hearing you speak gave me chills and a whole new outlook on life! I couldn't be happier with where I am right now and thank you for a small part of that!! I try to be the best friend I can be to myself every day. I thank you so much Russell—you're an inspiration to people everywhere!" WOW, right??

⇨ Lesson #106: Sharing others' quotes can inspire. No need to come up with everything yourself!

6/9—Today was the last day of a three day Life Coach Training course I taught. This was my second time teaching one. I am grateful for the opportunity (as always). There were 38 people in the class and I look forward to having many of them in my network going forward. The love in the room was palpable. They truly care about each other and enjoy being with one another. Best of all, they "walk the talk" and do things to keep the relationship fires burning—meeting up monthly, communicating via a Facebook group, etc. It is inspiring to see. I am ecstatic to be a new member of this circle of friends and colleagues.

⇨ Lesson #107: Stay connected to new, inspiring people that you meet. Folks come into our life for a reason and whatever you can do to build those new relationships—without sacrificing the good relationships in your life—will help enhance your experience on this Earth.

This is the halfway point of my book. I am proud that I've made it this far with six months' worth of things and people I'm grateful for—and 107 lessons so far for you. Here's to keeping up the inspiration!

What did you learn from this week's entries and what changes can you make to live your best life?

_____

_____

_____

_____

6/10—Today, I had lunch with my friend and former colleague Tammy Torres, or "TT" as I call her. We worked together for five years and were promoted to Manager the same day—July 1, 2007. The two of us also got to take a road trip to New Manager Training, which was a cool and fun experience. When you have a special bond with someone, you've obviously shared a lot with them—ups and downs in each other's lives, etc. Anyway, we were eating lunch, catching up, talking—it had been seemingly forever since we last met up—and at the end of the lunch she made an observation that I really appreciate. She said that she's noticed how much I've grown in the time we have known each other and how much more free and authentic I am these days. Wow. I had no idea that I made this transformation but she's right—I did! I am proud of myself, and I am thankful to her for pointing this out.

> ⇨ Lesson #108: As you think about those who are close to you, consider how they've changed for the better over the years and share this observation with them. I bet you'll make their day.

6/11—Last night, I got this note from Rebecca, a student in the Life Coach Training I just taught: "Thanks again for being in the room with us this weekend. Your presence and your energy were such a major contribution to my overall experience and it would have really been lacking without you there. I loved the way you smiled and engaged all the students with your eyes and gave us full attention when we were talking. You're an amazing active listener!" Wow! What a nice note!

> ⇨ Lesson #109: Be a great listener! Are you active—i.e. 100% engaged in what the person is saying and showing it? Do you make them feel as if they're the only person in the room AND in your thoughts? Are you being intuitive and seeing if there is 'more to the story' other than what they're saying?

6/12—I am grateful for the ease with which things happen sometimes. Every year in July or August, my Mom hosts a summer barbecue to celebrate my birthday, which is on August 12. I used to celebrate with my Aunt Marie every year. I was born on her 45th birthday and we marked the day we were both born every year until she passed away a few years ago. My Mom carries on the tradition though and we all treasure our fond memories of her. My grandmother died when I was in 9th grade so Aunt Marie was the matriarch of our family to many of us, or the 'chairman of the board' as my Mom always said.

Most years, trying to coordinate a date between me, my sister and my cousin Steve—who is like a brother to me and was Aunt Marie's grandson—is usually a bit challenging. We all have busy schedules and it typically takes a while to nail down a date in July or August. This year though is different! I texted my sister and Steve with a suggested date this afternoon. They both replied right away that it worked. Phew! I can't wait. There aren't as many family dinners as there used to be and as my friend Elaine Green says "It's always great to be around family." I'm especially excited to see Steve. These days we only get together a few times a year.

6/13—Last night, I had the first "All Hands" call for all the hosts on the Life Coach Radio Network. I asked them to come prepared with one question or idea. Oh my—they are smart and have many good ideas!

⇨ Lesson #110: Bring a group together to brainstorm. People like to share their wisdom on how something could be better. They're often insightful and everyone's experience will be enhanced as a result of asking.

6/14—I am grateful for the word "yet". I facilitated a workshop this evening and one of the participants made a statement that she isn't good at something. I said "How about adding the word *yet?* In other words, you're not good at it *yet?*" In the post-workshop evaluation, she wrote that adding these three little letters was the most significant thing she got out of the workshop! I love "yet" because it implies that you're working on it, that you're trending upward and that soon you WILL be good at it!

⇨ Lesson #111: In what aspect of your life can you add the word yet? For me, it's that I'm not a famous Life Coach YET! (If you tell your friends and family about the book though, maybe I will be!)

6/15—Today, I was working on the workshop that's ten days away with my friend, fellow Life Coach and collaboration partner Karen Collins. She has a totally different work style than me and I appreciate the rigor and added value she brings to this workshop that I had been giving by myself.

> ⇨ Lesson #112: Great minds think alike but people who think differently can likely accomplish more. Who in your circle thinks differently? How can you learn from them? This can include not just work situations but also personal. My close pal Charles Phillips is excellent at "things around the house" (picking out new items for the home—curtains, furniture, paint colors, etc.—and assembling things). I have little to no skills in this area, nor do I care to! Often, I have just asked him to handle everything, and he's happy to oblige. It's fun for him.

6/16—It's Fathers' Day! I'm thankful for Dads, especially the good ones, including mine (Russ Terry Sr.). I am also grateful when others organize things. One step better is when they organize and pay for things! My Mom and her longtime companion Tom O'Donnell reserve two weeks at the Jersey Shore every year. They select the weeks (always in June and September), book the houses, bring sheets, towels, etc.—and pay for it. It is lovely to just 'show up' and know that I'll spend quality time with our immediate family and Tom's. His son Sean O'Donnell is like a stepbrother to me and is fun to be around. By the way, I'm not a bump on a log. I usually contribute in some other way. Last year, I made Dads' day dinner for everyone and breakfast the next morning. This year, I just made breakfast but on Fathers' Day I did suggest that "all the non-Dad adults" (which includes me) pay for our big group dinner at our favorite beach-side restaurant.

> ⇨ Lesson #113: What event can you organize for family, friends, co-workers, etc.? I'm not saying become an event planner or anything but a couple things throughout the year is a good, reasonable number that will bring enjoyment to many. You don't have to spend a lot of money. A potluck dinner, or a game night at your home, are both great examples of events that don't cost much but will bring enjoyment to many.

What did you learn from this week's entries and what changes can you make to live your best life?

_____

_____

_____

_____

6/17—I'm grateful there are more and more places with gluten free options. I ended up having several gluten free meals while here at the Jersey Shore for these few days. It's lovely to have pizza, pancakes, etc.—foods I normally can't eat. They're delicious.

6/18—Someone let me merge in front of them today! This seems minor but I was thankful. Some drivers are . . . somewhat jerk-like . . . as if being one car closer to the front of traffic is going to make any difference whatsoever.

⇨ Lesson #114: Let someone merge. It's a nice way to live.

6/19—I recently decided to recruit new hosts on the Life Coach Radio Network and got FOUR in the span of 24 hours. Wow! If you build it, they will come.

6/20—I am grateful for the sand and the ocean. I had a great time at the shore this week with my niece and nephew (Julia and Sean). Being at the beach is an easy, free (depending where you go) thing that many people—kids especially—enjoy. They spent hours and hours searching for sand crabs, making sand castles—and of course getting sand ALL over them. It's a neat thing to watch and be a part of. I can't mention the beach though without also imparting some advice . . .

⇨ Lesson #115: Wear sunscreen!! Apply liberally and often. Don't miss any spots. Ask someone to put it on your back. Also, don't rely on the spray stuff if it's windy and doesn't actually get on you!

6/21—Today, I decided to co-chair a charitable event with my friend and fellow Life Coach Danielle Mund. She too has celiac disease and we want to do something to raise money to help find a cure and help people deal with managing gluten allergies. Volunteerism and giving back is SO important to me. For more than six years, I was very involved with Big Brothers Big Sisters—as a Big Brother to three boys/young men. Eventually, one went away to college and the other two decided to quit the program this past fall. Over the last nine months, I "got busy" and wasn't as involved in any volunteer efforts (after having devoted a lot of free time to it for so long). I appreciate Danielle asking me to do this with her. I hope that we raise a lot of money and put on a great event that many people will want to attend.

6/22—I got 12 more hosts on the radio network this week! We're up to about 40. I can't believe it. I am excited that the idea I had about three months ago has become popular quickly, and is wildly exceeding my own lofty expectations.

6/23—I'm grateful for being in the right place at the right time. Earlier this week I broke a string in my racket playing tennis (but still won the point yay). I hadn't gotten a chance to figure out where and how to get it restrung. Then all of a sudden in today's match my opponent broke his string. He knew of a place that handles it and said he'd drop mine off for me! Isn't that great? All I had to do was pick up the racket (and pay for it of course).

What did you learn from this week's entries and what changes can you make to live your best life?

_____

_____

_____

_____

6/24—I am grateful today for finding a parking spot. I know I've mentioned this one before, but we are talking New York City on a blazing hot day, and this baby was in the shade!! To locate a spot and have my black car not be scalding hot when I returned to it, (*after* playing tennis for two hours in the heat,) was nothing short of a miracle! Can I get an AMEN?

6/25—I facilitated an amazing workshop tonight with Karen Collins. Wow. I learned so much from her. My workshops were good or great but collaborating with her has given my work new dimension. The feedback from the 24 participants was outstanding. Our goal was to have 20 people and we exceeded it. I had to run out this morning and rent more chairs! Everything came together nicely: being able to pull up outside (a rarity in NYC) to drop off the 14 extra chairs we needed; my pal Mike Rivera walking up as I arrived and him helping me carry them up a few flights of stairs in the heat; a free parking spot around the corner (another NYC rarity); and the attendees really enjoying interacting with each other—even when matched with someone they didn't know (which was one of Karen's ideas to help them step outside their comfort zone).

⇨ Lesson #116: Tear a page out of Karen's book! Step outside your comfort zone in some way.

6/26—I was out with Karen and other Life Coaches last night to send her off for her big move to Seattle in a few days. Also my friend John Leonardo and his family are moving to Toronto. Many times when close friends move away, people are sad, hurt, not supportive, etc. I have a different view. I am happy for my friends that they're about to embark on a next chapter. I know they didn't make this decision lightly and trust that it's right for them. I'm excited to see what's next in their lives. With Facebook, texting, email, Skype, etc., someone being far away literally doesn't mean they're far figuratively. My BFF Colee Schroeder moved away one year ago this weekend. She is so happy in her new life in Minneapolis—promoted at work, purchased a house, and most importantly, close to her family in their new city of residence.

⇨ Lesson #117: Be happy for friends and family members who move away (or even co-workers who leave for a new job). It can be a lonely and/or stressful time. Once they've departed, do your best to contact them whenever they're in your thoughts. I bet they'll appreciate it. Visit them if you can.

6/27—Yesterday, I was playing tennis at Ft. Greene Park in Brooklyn. I noticed many wonderful things around me: a grandfather and grandson playing together on the court next to us (and really enjoying it), the smell of flowers, a graduate and her family posing for a picture. Experiencing these three things put a smile on my face. I can't explain why exactly but they just gave me a warm feeling in my heart.

⇨ Lesson #118: Notice things around you. Simple things can be inspiring and beautiful.

6/28—Today, I'm grateful that our radio shows got uploaded to iTunes—free podcasts for everyone! All 48 shows we've done so far are there! Modern technology is wonderful, as are more people being exposed to our content—especially in a free and convenient manner.

6/29—Oprah. Need I say more? I will anyway. She has done so much for so many people and her work continues with her own TV network (appropriately named OWN). In particular these days, her Super Soul Sunday shows are exposing the masses to more spiritual content. I think she's part of a shift that's going on in society.

6/30—Yesterday, at my softball tournament, a teammate who didn't know anyone brought food and beverages for everyone. What a kind-hearted guy! I'm glad he did because I was hungry and thirsty as the day wore on.

⇨ Lesson #119: When is your next opportunity to be kind-hearted? Will you seize this chance?

What did you learn from this week's entries and what changes can you make to live your best life?

_____

_____

_____

_____

7/1—Yesterday, I took part in the Walk From Obesity. I'm grateful that my parents raised me to eat healthy. Obesity often leads to chronic illnesses.

⇨ Lesson #120: If you're a family who is raising someone, do everything in your power to stop any cycle of fatty foods that you grew up with and replace them with fresh vegetables, fruits and other non-processed foods, while still getting enough protein and 'good carbs' such as brown rice, sweet potatoes and quinoa.

7/2—I got a nice poem from the previously-mentioned Luis Nunez yesterday. Here it is:

May this month bring you satisfaction, peace and joy
May all the desires of your heart be granted
May this be the beginning of new things in your life
Stay strong, be positive and fulfill your dreams.

Isn't that nice? Poets are so wise. My favorite is Maya Angelou. The best quote from her is "People may not remember what you said or what you did, but they will always remember how you made them feel." I agree 100%.

⇨ Lesson #121: How are YOU making people feel? Good? Better as a result of their interaction with you? I hope so.

7/3—Today, I drove back from a trip to Montreal to visit Joachim and am grateful for two things:

1) The sun—during most of my trips there this year, it's been raining or snowing, including my way up on Monday, when there was a torrential downpour. But today the wonderful sun was shining so bright! It enables us to do so much. I can play sports outside, kids can get out of the house and enjoy their friends, we can all get our Vitamin D, etc. A nice sunny day makes many of us feel good.

2) Those signs on highways that tell you what food and gas options are at each of the exits. This is the best invention ever! As someone who is health conscious but also gluten free, my options to eat on the go are very limited. However, there's ONE "quick but not fast food" option—a Panera Bread—on the six hour drive. I was SO happy to see the sign. I've never wanted a nutritious, delicious salad so badly!

⇨ Lesson #122: If you make a long car ride often, make a note of where the best food and cheapest gas options are (and keep the note in your car). In addition to the Panera, the gas at this exit is more than 20 cents a gallon cheaper than most other stops along my route. Exit 19 on I-87 is #1 in my book!

7/4—I love swimming pools. Today was the fourth of July and I spent it with my BFF Anika Johnson and her family. Her apartment building has a pool. It's a great gathering place for relaxation, catching up and cooling down. Even though I've seen her in many other settings in the last eight months, this was my first trip to her home since Hurricane Sandy. It brought back memories of what a challenging experience that was. However, I also have great memories of her putting me up for two days while I was without electricity. During that time, I was able to bond with her adorable daughter. If it wasn't for the storm, it's unlikely I would have gone over there for two days. Little Angelica and I had fun in the pool together today. I'm grateful that our extra time together in the fall—forced upon me due to the storm—was the conduit to quality time with Angelica, and enabled her to be quite comfortable around me more than eight months later.

⇨ Lesson #123: Look for the positive in bad situations. I promise there is one—or more.

7/5—Today, I arrived at the annual Essence Festival in New Orleans. This is my fourth straight year coming. It's an incredible time—the highlight of a highlight-filled year. It features dozens of artists in concert, celebrities available for meet-and-greets and pictures, and stimulating intellectual discussions at its Empowerment conference. Congratulations to Essence Magazine for putting on an amazing event. If you're ever able to attend, I highly recommend it. I must say too that New Orleans is finally closer to a full recovery since Hurricane Katrina. This is the most crowded I've ever seen the festival. Crime is down significantly. People are noticing that the city and the atmosphere are different here than in prior years.

7/6—Tonight, I saw many performances at Essence but the one that stands out most is singer Jody Watley. She had a ton of hits many years ago (Looking for a New Love, Friends, etc.) and the former Solid Gold dancer is now reinvigorating her career at age 54. It is inspiring to see someone her age singing, dancing, practically jumping around on stage. I normally feel like I can do ANYTHING and watching her perform made me feel like I can do even *more than anything*. I am glad that I saw her.

⇨ Lesson #124: You can do whatever you set your mind to— regardless of your age!

7/7—Beyonce. Enough said right? I am grateful she EXISTS and is who she is. Her concert tonight was the grand finale of another great Essence Fest. This performance was the best I've ever been to in my life. She gives so much on stage, she has such a huge catalog of great songs to sing, so many people love her, etc. This was the biggest crowd in the 19 year history of the festival. I'm so glad I got to be a part of it. Wow.

What did you learn from this week's entries and what changes can you make to live your best life?

_____

_____

_____

_____

7/8—I had a great day in New Orleans today. Usually I fly back on Monday but this year the flights were much cheaper departing on Tuesday so we stayed an extra day. I got to do so many things that, otherwise, I wouldn't have done. One was talking to my wing-man Craig Washington about his time in the Air Force in Afghanistan and the friends he lost. Ever since he mentioned them at his birthday party on Memorial Day weekend, I had been wondering 'what their story was'—where they were from, how it happened and so on. Without the hustle and bustle of the events, we had time to sit down and have a nice, long conversation about it. I'm glad we did. I know that story will stay with me for the rest of my life.

7/9—This was our last day in New Orleans. I am grateful for the city's generosity. Many of the retailers (especially the candy stores) offer FREE samples! Oh my word, if you've never had a praline, you may want to put this book down just long enough to find out how you can get them delivered to you as soon as possible. It's the best candy ever! I think we got free pralines in about five different candy stores! Can you tell I have a sweet tooth? Needless to say, I bought some for the trip home.

⇨ Lesson #125: Be generous. It feels good and is simply the right thing to do. Also, many times when you show generosity, doing so will come back to you and then some.

7/10—I want to pause here to recognize Craig for being a great wing man—in life and on trips. We've probably all been in situations where we traveled with people and it was an unpleasant experience. I know I have. Craig however is cool, calm and collected, and he laughs at ALL the funny things I say LOL. We had many great laughs the last five days. Also, the handling the money situation went smoothly. (I paid for the hotel and then he had to pay me.) Again, that's a situation that can be awkward. With him, it's not.

⇨ Lesson #126: If you want to travel with others, consider taking a short trip (one or two nights, somewhat local perhaps) before you invest in a lot of money to go somewhere far with them for a longer vacation.

7/11—Cheese curls! I know this may not be as deep as some of my other entries but darn they're just so delicious and addicting. I may even want to add potato chips to the list of things I'm grateful for. I want to say though that I don't eat these foods often. Instead, they're a treat once in a while.

⇨ Lesson #127: It's fine to indulge sometimes in snacks that aren't the most nutritious, as long as you do it in moderation. The best times to have them are: as a reward for accomplishing something and/or early enough in the day so you can burn off the calories.

7/12—Being trusted and having people I can trust is a wonderful thing. I had a session this afternoon with a friend and potential client. Little does he know he actually moved me to tears! (It happens to me often—good tears as in "Wow! I'm having an incredibly positive impact on this person's life"). He said he TRUSTS me and if he wasn't having sessions with me he probably wouldn't have them with anyone—and thus not moving his life from functional to optimal. Isn't that a beautiful thing? Who do YOU trust? Even more importantly . . . who trusts YOU?

⇨ Lesson #128: What are you doing (or how are you living your life in a way) that establishes you as someone that people feel comfortable confiding in—without judgment?

7/13—I had a radio show with two new hosts today. I'm thankful that I can do it well with little preparation. That's a skill and I'm glad I have it. The show was the premiere for my second radio network (International Life Coach Radio) and the ratings were higher than all but one show on the flagship station (Life Coach Radio Network).

⇨ Lesson #129: What's a skill you have that does not require a ton of time or effort to do it well? How can you spend more of your life doing those things?

7/14—This morning I had a tennis match and I appreciate the good sportsmanship of my opponent (Nat Rew). There was a ball on my side that was probably out but I couldn't tell. (For those of you who don't know the rules, you're responsible for making the in/out calls on your side of the court.) Because I wasn't sure, I didn't call it out, but he said "no that's fine it was out". He didn't have to do that but it's nice and classy that he did.

What did you learn from this week's entries and what changes can you make to live your best life?

_____

_____

_____

_____

7/15—Today, I am grateful for grace—someone either saying a personal one before a meal and/or exhibiting it in a certain situation. Nothing against the graces a lot of us said growing up, but for me personally, because I've repeated them so many times over the years, they've lost their meaning to some extent. I love the good old fashioned let's hold hands and just speak from the heart instead.

As for the showing grace kind, I am always reminded of men's tennis player James Blake. He suffered some great hardships in his life—death of his Dad at a young age, a debilitating injury—and on the back cover of his book *Breaking Back*, Hall of Famer Andre Agassi said "We all encounter adversity in our lives. The real reflection of character is how we deal with it. The grace and dignity that James has shown during some very difficult times has been a source of great inspiration." Are you exhibiting grace when faced with adversity?

7/16—I'm thankful I have an understanding nature, and that people appreciate it. Today, I got two emails in a row that said "thanks for understanding". In general, I don't make a big deal about things and try my best to diffuse any situations—or at least not be mad, upset, frustrated, etc.

⇨ Lesson #130: How are YOU being understanding as issues come up at work, at home, in relationships, etc.? What can you do better?

7/17—People who keep track of time are excellent. I'm often the one who is up front speaking in certain group situations, or running from meeting to meeting on a typical day in the city. Having someone who takes pride in making sure I stay on schedule is a dream come true. I'm usually good about watching the clock but when another person does it for me (like my friend and colleague did today), it's much appreciated.

⇨ Lesson #131: In what situations can you help someone keep time? At work when a colleague or boss is making a presentation? In social situations when you know a super busy friend has to leave by a certain time to be prompt for their next commitment?

7/18—Thank goodness for air conditioning! It was hot, humid, sticky, muggy, oppressive, etc. today. You name the gross adjective and it fit. I was happy to be inside teaching Life Coach Training (with amazing people as always) and not out and about sweating my behind off!

7/19—I am always happy when a restaurant gives me quick service! Today my gal pal Carrie Fiore Andrews and I went to a "nice chain restaurant that they have at mall entrances" (you can probably guess which one I'm talking about LOL). We were in and out in 45 minutes, which was much less than I expected and much appreciated on a super hectic day.

7/20—I'm grateful for time to run errands!! (I'm such a nerd right? "I am super-excited to run errands!") It had been WEEKS since I was able to go to the bank. I was carrying around three checks to cash. (That reminds me—I want to download my bank's mobile app!) I also desperately needed a new hand towel for the bathroom and groceries from a couple different stores. It just goes to show you though: even loathsome activities to some can be welcome things to others. It's all just a matter of perspective.

⇨ Lesson #132: What's a good way to look at errands (or even household chores for that matter)? Maybe relief and/or a sense of accomplishment that you had time to do them?

7/21—A beautiful sunset is a wonderful thing. Tonight, I was sitting by the Hudson River in Chelsea Piers Park in NYC, overlooking New Jersey. All of a sudden during my meeting I had to say "I am sorry will you excuse me I just need to take a picture of the sun setting over the water". I quickly posted it to Instagram and Facebook and got more than 50 Likes, which was a lot for me at the time.

What did you learn from this week's entries and what changes can you make to live your best life?

_____

_____

_____

_____

7/22—My Mom got her mammogram results today—and she had a clean bill of health!

⇨ Lesson #133: If you're a woman of a certain age, get tested for breast cancer at the frequency you're supposed to. If you know someone who fits that description, make sure they're on top of this and getting their screenings.

7/23—I am grateful to wake up every day. (This one is borrowed from Maya Angelou, whom as I said before I adore.) Isn't this a wonderful thing? Life is great and I'm glad I experience more and more of it each passing day.

7/24—I often smile when I see a smile on a stranger. Today, I was walking through a parking lot and witnessed a young woman laughing exuberantly at something the male driver said. It brings me great joy to see others happy—people I know and people I don't!

7/25—I appreciate when two people give you the same piece of advice! It's almost like God's way of saying "you should do this. Can I be any clearer??" It happened to me in late 2011/early 2012, when two friends and colleagues suggested I become a Life Coach (which has worked out FANTASTIC—thank you Lora Boltniew and Tamarra Causley Robinson!!) Here's another recent example: my health insurance went up about $35 a month and I was contemplating switching to the cheaper one but luckily I saw friends Shachi Doshi yesterday and Joanne Ryan today and they both recommended that I keep it as is. I'm glad I did. I don't mind taking risks in life but with something like this it's probably better to be conservative, especially given all the sports I play and the risk for potential injury.

⇨ Lesson #134: When two people separately give you the same advice, take it as a strong sign from God and follow it!

7/26—Today, my International Life Coach Radio colleague Annette Johnson said "you ask really great questions Russ". It's nice of her to say that. I do take great pride in my active listening skills and being in the moment and trusting my intuition with what to ask as a follow-up based on what someone just said. Even though she shared this with me in the context of our appearance together on the radio, it's relevant in all walks of life. I already made it a lesson back on May 6th but it's worth repeating that we each have two ears and one mouth. In an ideal scenario you listen 2/3 of the time and talk 1/3 of the time.

7/27—My softball team and I had a walk off win today!! (For non-sports fans, this is when the home team scores the winning run in the bottom of the last inning and everyone on both teams "walks off" the field.) This was the first time I have ever experienced it in all my years of playing. Oh my word, I was SO excited. I was on first base and I ran to second, then the winning run scored and I ran toward home, then I ran toward first base to hug my teammate Stan who had the game-winning hit. I was running in circles and it felt great! I picked him up in the air!

7/28—I saw a sign today about the 2014 Special Olympics being here in New Jersey. I posted something about it on Facebook and quite a few of my friends are going to volunteer with me. I am glad I stumbled upon the sign, and that people I am close to are inspired to participate with me. Events such as these can be amazing life experiences. It's almost a gift to volunteer!

What did you learn from this week's entries and what changes can you make to live your best life?

_____

_____

_____

_____

7/29—I am super grateful for things working out, especially when I am "heavily scheduled" which is often the case. Yesterday I had a tennis match then a radio show. It is amazing that I beat my tough opponent, much less in barely enough time to get to my friend and colleague Jay Cadet's in time to do our show. Sometimes the stars align perfectly. It only took me 15 minutes to drive from the park by Yankee Stadium to his place in Harlem (and find a parking spot). Phew!

7/30—Angela Birchett. She's one of the amazing singers at the aforementioned Monday Soul Night at Toshi's. Seeing her perform is inspiring. Many, many people marvel at her talent. She puts so much energy into every performance. On top of that, she's the sweetest, nicest person ever. We live near each other and take turns driving and taking the other home. She entertains me then chauffeurs me. What a sweet deal!

7/31—The radio show hosts on my networks are REALLY ENJOYING working together, meeting each other, sharing knowledge, etc. This thing that I created a few months ago is actually enhancing people's lives! I've taken people who didn't know each other and provided a forum for them to interact, learn, grow and love. It's an amazing thing to watch.

⇨ Lesson #135: What can you do to create an "Everybody wins" situation?

8/1—I have an injury (bruised butt cheek from a softball slide LOL). It's been more than a month so I finally went to the doctor. He recommended I swim as a non-contact form of exercise. I posted something about needing a pool to swim at on Facebook and many people provided great ideas. One was a gym less than a mile from me. It's cheap and was a great workout! I was breathing SO heavy! It's yet another example of an alleged "bad" thing (in this case the injury) being the facilitator to a lovely new experience! I see this being a new regular activity of mine. I just wrote earlier this month about how can you look at "bad" situations and instead turn them into a positive? Therefore the lesson today is:

⇨ Lesson #136: When you need advice, recommendations, etc. on a certain situation, posting your question or issue to Facebook is an excellent way to seek input. I can't tell you how many times I've done this! People are often willing to take a minute to share their experience.

8/2—Lessons learned are a beautiful thing! Starting today, I am dog-sitting for the next five days. It is NOT going smoothly. I won't bore you with the gross details but now I know that this is not my area of expertise and I should think long and hard before saying YES next time.

⇨ Lesson #137: Feel empowered to say NO thank you.

8/3—I am grateful when people are open to feedback, especially the unsolicited kind. I had to give some to one of the hosts on my radio networks and she was totally cool about it. I am so relieved! I was a bit worried how she would respond. I shouldn't have been!

⇨ Lesson #138: As long as feedback is delivered in a nice (but direct) way and with the intention of helping, give it with confidence (and swiftness so that the situation doesn't go too long without being corrected).

8/4—Recently, I made a bet with my new friend/protégé Linton Gooden. (We bet on who would do better guessing the answers on an episode of *Wheel of Fortune*. Given my experience on the show, I was destined to win!) The loser had to make dinner and I collected on it tonight. We invited a couple of his friends over and made a fun little gathering out of it. All four of us had a great time.

⇨ Lesson #139: Figure out who you can "make a bet" with. The winner has to do something for the other that you can both enjoy.

What did you learn from this week's entries and what changes can you make to live your best life?

_____

_____

_____

_____

8/5—Today is my last day of dog sitting (mercifully). I was rushing to take them out before I had an hour session with a client. I got a few blocks from our home and realized I forgot paper towels and/or a bag to pick up . . . their bowel movements. They didn't "do it" every time I walked them but of course BOTH of them went this time. Ugh! What was I going to do? Well, thank goodness for ANGELS! I truly believe they exist. A lady was walking by. I asked her "by any chance do you have a tissue or a piece of scrap paper in your purse?" She didn't, but she did have about six paper towels, which she happily handed me. It was a summer miracle. Who carries paper towels in their purse?! I sure am glad she does—or at least did that day.

8/6—I was fortunate to be featured in a YouTube video series by a colleague (James Singleton). The episode—on failure—aired today. This may sound crazy but I'm grateful for failure. Without it, greater levels of success aren't possible. There are always lessons that come from it. I even ventured to say that failure doesn't even exist (but I'll leave that discussion for a future book)!

⇨ Lesson #140: Fail often. You'll not only be fine but it's likely you'll be better off for it, as these events usually get you closer to where you want to be.

8/7—I love the song Poison by Bell Biv Devoe. It's my favorite karaoke jam. Every time I hear it I smile even more than usual. It came on tonight while I was doing dishes. What a perfect time to be energized—when doing a not-so-exciting activity. My favorite line in it is "Never trust a big butt and a smile!" So funny!!

8/8—I flew to New Orleans this evening. Tomorrow, I am speaking at the Alpha Kappa Psi fraternity's biennial conference. As I mentioned back in January when this opportunity was a possibility, I am excited because this is my most high profile presentation to date. It's my first national speaking gig. I intend to make sure many more opportunities such as this are in my future.

8/9—My "Live Your Best Life" presentation went great today. Every seat was taken. People were standing, sitting on the floor, coming up to me afterward wanting to take a photo with me, like I was a celebrity or something! Am I a celebrity?! Or at least becoming one? If so, how cool! People appreciated the content. I love the moment of having hundreds of eyes on me and helping them have that 'a-ha' moment where the light bulb goes off and they realize that they want to start living life a different way!

8/10—At the conference yesterday, they gave me some gifts of appreciation, which I appreciate: A Starbucks gift card and two little books with wise and/or inspirational sayings. I am always looking for content to share on my social media (Twitter, Instagram, Facebook, etc.) and I bet they don't realize how much they've helped me by giving me these tokens of their thanks.

⇨ Lesson #141: Give little gifts. A little bit goes a long way.

8/11—Joachim went through a lot to visit NYC for my birthday. On the way down from Montreal he got stopped and detained at the border! They kept him with customs for about 90 minutes and the last bus to NYC left without him. He therefore had to sleep in a chair in the office until the first bus left the next morning. A lesser man would have said "I am sorry Russ but I cannot make it for your birthday." He is a man of his word though, and he persevered and finally arrived about 16 hours after he left home. (As comparison, it usually takes me about six hours to drive up there.) I am grateful that he made it and appreciative that he's such a good man who would do something like that for me. It's worth repeating the lesson from February 18th: when someone visits you from out-of-town, treat them like royalty. Traveling is often exhausting, challenging, etc. and they'll appreciate you 'rolling out the red carpet'.

What did you learn from this week's entries and what changes can you make to live your best life?

_____

_____

_____

_____

8/12—Today is my birthday! Woohoo! I am excited for another year on this Earth not just living but thriving! I got many notes and calls from people. Here are a few of the best:

Save-worthy voicemail from my Mom—singing happy birthday, remembering how happy she was to have a baby (I am the older of her two children) and that she can't believe it's been 42 years. I was thinking to myself "I wish I could have been there to witness how happy she was" and then I realized I was LOL. Too bad I can't remember anything from that day!

My cousin Steven Lowry, who as I've mentioned before is like a brother to me, texted about how he was telling one of his friends about me: "Gave him a history of your working days, and the different paths you have taken, the bravery of stepping out and taking chances and how you succeed in all you do! I'm proud of you, cuz. You follow your dreams; not many do. Fear keeps us in our comfort zones." He is incredibly wise and insightful. I love listening to what he has to say.

My friend Alex Casthely: "Wishing you the best and happiest of birthdays. The world was made a much better place on this day, 42 years ago when you entered it. You are truly an exceptional man and I'm glad to call you a friend." Wow right? I'm grateful for Alex. He's an amazing supporter of me and my projects.

Bert Gervais, who I met once almost 18 months ago: "I wanted to wish you a Happy Birthday! You are truly the type of person who leaves a place better than they found it and I admire that about you." I never thought about this before but what he describes is my mission in life. It's awesome that Bert picked up on that even though we've only been in each other's company once.

⇨ Lesson #142: When you wish someone a happy birthday, do more than just that. Send them a few lines of what specifically is special about them. It takes less than a minute, but I bet what you say will stand out to them and make them feel great about themselves.

⇨ Lesson #143: Make repeating entries in your calendar for people's birthdays. It's on Facebook but sometimes we may not see it, or maybe they don't have an account. We lose touch with many people but birthdays are a great day—and way—to reconnect.

8/13—I had a big birthday party last night! It was incredibly fun. About 30-40 people came out to celebrate with me, on a Monday night no less! I am honored they were there and excited that so many people said they had such a great time. I held it at the previously-mentioned Soul Night at Toshi's and my new friends serenaded me!! Angela Birchett sang Sweet Thing (by Chaka Khan and also Mary J. Blige) and said "Where is Russell??" so that I could come up in front of the stage before she sang. Also, the Soul Night band learned how to play the Stevie Wonder version of Happy Birthday, which was awesomely sung by the hostess with the mostest Shira Elias. Both of these lovely ladies are Leos too. We're all born within two weeks of each other. Wait! Let me rephrase since I'm much older than them LOL. Our birthdays are within two weeks of each other! One last thing: my friends Ayanna Lee, Maisha Husband and I danced to so many songs. Dancing feels great. What an excellent way to express joy, have fun . . . and work up a sweat!

⇨ Lesson #144: Throw a birthday party for yourself! It's a great opportunity to bring friends together and have fun. Who here doesn't want that?

8/14—Today, I am grateful for precision. I've been playing a lot of tennis matches lately and some of my shots are 'winners' that go exactly where I want them to!

8/15—I'm thankful for good luck charms. I had an amazing comeback this afternoon at tennis! I was down 3-6, 2-5 when a woman walked onto the next court (which had been empty). She cheered us on for a bit while waiting for her opponent and that must have been the luck and/or motivation I needed. After she arrived, I won five straight games and took the second set 7-5 and then won the super tiebreaker third set 10-5! That was my biggest comeback EVER in 25-30 years of playing! It was also against my rival Gregg Leib, who gave me my only regular season loss last year. Comebacks are amazing—in sports but also in life.

⇨ Lesson #145: If you're down, don't count yourself out. Pick yourself up, and put the pedal to the metal to make your life not just great, but even better than it was before. Trust me everyone involved loves a great comeback, AND everyone has been down at some point in their life.

8/16—I've said this before but I am appreciative of people who have skills in areas other than mine. Today's example is my fellow coach and Life Coach Radio Networks colleague Filomena Iorio-Tasoluk. She's worked tirelessly in recent months to create our LCRNs website, which we launched today. (You can check it out at www. lifecoachradionetworks.com). It looks fantastic and we received lots of great feedback. As I've mentioned before, great minds think alike but different minds get more done! I never would have been able to do this on my own and/or without her.

8/17—I am grateful for carpooling. I love win/win situations and this is one of them. This morning, I drove my fellow Philadelphia native and fellow Jersey City resident Randy Williams to our softball playoffs. The games are located in a hard-to-get-to-by-train spot so I was happy to help him out. It was great learning more about him, and he paid money for tolls, which I gladly accepted! We may have lost our games that day but we both won from a great life experience standpoint.

⇨ Lesson #146: What's a situation coming up soon where you can carpool with someone? It saves money and is an all-around good time.

8/18—My third radio network—the Life Coach Chat Channel— premiered today. So far thousands of people have tuned in to my idea and dozens of coaches are using it as a platform to enhance their profiles. I'm proud of what I have built and will continue building. I am also thankful that it resonates with Coaches and the public. One last thing: it's a much-needed, additional revenue stream for me!

What did you learn from this week's entries and what changes can you make to live your best life?

_____

_____

_____

_____

8/19—Last week while he was here, Joachim gave me a stern "talking to" about my driving. (There were a couple situations during his visit that led to this much-needed discussion.) Because I drive solo so much, I am ashamed to say I hadn't realized that I was taking risks here and there and not being as cautious as I should have been. I am not proud of this BUT I am glad he had the courage to say something to me about it, and I'm grateful that I listened and *heard* him. I have vowed to change.

⇨ Lesson #147: If someone in your life needs a stern talking to, do it. On the other hand, if you are on the receiving end of it, be open to it and take it as a wake-up call.

8/20—I'm always glad when things end early. Tonight, I had a conference call with the radio show hosts and not everyone joined so it allowed me to go home after the call and before a radio show appearance. (Otherwise I would have been hidden in a hotel's conference room for three hours trying to speak from a quiet space.) I swear sometimes my schedule is crazy. Speaking of that, check out the next entry:

8/21—I may forget things here and there but today I am thankful for all that I DO remember. I had a crazy day today in Manhattan—a tennis match, shower and change into casual clothes, a Skype session with a potential radio show host, visiting a friend who just had a baby, a workshop I was delivering (and dress clothes for that), a movie premiere, etc. Needless to say, I had a lot of stuff to pack and shockingly brought everything I needed!

8/22—This morning I had to come back from a set down to beat my tennis opponent. What's up with all these comebacks lately?! Can I please start winning in straight sets again?? Anyway, he complimented me on my mental stamina. I am glad that I possess it and use it!

⇨ Lesson #148: It's hard to have mental toughness (on the court and in life) but if you can sustain your intensity and drive until you reach your goal(s), you will be incredibly happy and proud of yourself that you did.

8/23—Today, I'm proud that I'm considerate and thoughtful and that others appreciate these qualities. One great way you can live an optimal life and enhance the quality of another person's life is by heeding my next lesson:

⇨ Lesson #149: Remember people (friends, family members, etc.) on the anniversary of the day they lost a loved one.

EVERY time I text or email someone with a simple 'thinking of you today', the person is incredibly grateful, touched, etc. It's easy to recall a birthday but with a repeating entry in your calendar you can remember these days too. A close friend lost her brother on this day a couple years ago, and here's what she had to say when I emailed her today: "Russ, I can't tell you how much this message means to me. Today is his anniversary and I've been sad and thinking about it all week but to turn it into a happy occasion, I'm calling today his new soul's birthday. I really appreciate you remembering . . . these days are difficult. I'll try to do the same for others since I know how good it felt to receive your message—sometimes I wonder if it's easier to act like it didn't happen but I know that will never happen. Thanks Russ!! Love you! :-)" I love her too.

8/24—Zoos are a fun activity for all ages. I went today with my sister, my brother-in-law John Reavy and the kids. The five of us had a great time bonding. There are some fascinating sights there. The animals keep the kids interested for hours at a time, which is hard to do! I'm glad these exist so that kids of all ages (including grown-ups) can enjoy them.

8/25—This may sound simple, but I am thankful for the sound of an automatic key unlocking my car! For the last few months, I haven't had an automatic key. One was lost on a flight to San Juan and the other broke from overuse, so I have had to fumble with a manual key to load and unload my car, lock and unlock the doors, etc. Modern technology is awesome and makes our lives much more convenient! This time, without the benefit of it, has made me so thankful it exists.

⇨ Lesson #150: Think about what your favorite modern conveniences are, what your life was like before them and how appreciative you are to have what you have now.

What did you learn from this week's entries and what changes can you make to live your best life?

_____

_____

_____

_____

8/26—The latest thing I am grateful for is traveling! This afternoon, I arrived in Provincetown, Massachusetts, a cozy little town in Cape Cod. I've never been to this area before and it's always nice to see new parts of the world! It's quaint here. I've heard a lot about it and I am glad I am finally checking it out. Those of us who are fortunate enough to have the time and money to travel are lucky. I bet many people take vacations for granted. I sure don't.

⇨ Lesson #151: Appreciate being able to travel. Many people can't, for various reasons.

⇨ Lesson #152: Take your vacation time, even if it's a "stay-cation"! Did you know that more than half of all Americans don't use all their allotted time off? That's a shame. We need vacations to refresh, recharge and de-stress.

8/27—I love meeting, connecting with, bonding with and just plain old having fun with new people. My close pal Joe Dudash organized this week, meaning he picked the house, figured out who would stay in it, etc. The other guy in our rental is his friend Steve Pessagno, who I had never met. That could have gone poorly, but Steve and I had fun getting to know each other. We have a lot in common, plus he makes me laugh all the time! Joe showed great instincts that we would get along so well.

⇨ Lesson #153: Think about your circle of friends and consider who would appreciate being introduced to each other.

8/28—I launched another new venture—the Life Coach TV Network, with two of my Life Coach Radio Network colleagues (Danielle Mercurio and Andrea Ruchelman). We announced it today and already have a lot of interest, which I am thankful for and excited about. One of my awesome friends—Wayne Wilson—posted the following on my Facebook about it. I'm inspired by what he said and I hope you are too:

"Again, I have to say how great I think it is how much you're doing and growing your business . . . Really an inspiration to a lot of people as to what someone can do and how they can move their life in a different direction when they're really committed to an idea!"

His note is so nice! I also must give an honorable mention to Danielle for calling us "Oprah's NextGen Squad". I couldn't agree more!

8/29—This may sound odd, but I am grateful I spent a lot of money this week in Provincetown. It was more than I thought it would be but it has me more motivated than ever to pursue revenue-generating activities now that I am back home. My new philosophy: "pedal to the metal" (as in step on it!)

⇨ Lesson #154: What's your main priority in your life and are you 'pedal to the metal' with it? Don't let things scare or distract you from going for what you want with a (good) vengeance.

8/30—I got my butt kicked in tennis today! I am glad though. It showed that I am not perfect and that I have some things to work on if I want to successfully defend my title, make it to the Finals in the fall and win. I plan to do just that and will spend time working on my game in the coming weeks and months.

8/31—I am thankful for publicists, specifically MINE! I met with her for the first time today and we had SUCH a productive session. She has some excellent ideas about how I can do an even better job than I already am of spreading the word about me and the services I offer.

9/1—I realized today that the kids upstairs have been away for the summer. I am not sure how I didn't know because, at their age, they make a lot of noise. Regardless, I am glad that I didn't have to hear them stomping around the last few months. (By the way, just to be clear, I love kids. My niece and nephew—whom I love dearly—are the same age as my neighbors so I know what children are like at that age. They're fun and lovely, just sometimes it's a bit much when it feels like they're running around on my head. At 7am . . . on a weekend!)

What did you learn from this week's entries and what changes can you make to live your best life?

_____

_____

_____

_____

9/2—Today, I finished my tennis regular season in first place with a 27-2 record! I am excited that I persevered through some tough matches and now, I am on to the playoffs! My goal is to win the championship just like last year and, as you've hopefully realized in reading this book, I am serious about my goals, whether they're work-related or personal. I am going to work hard these next couple months to maintain my level of play with the hopes of making it to (and winning) the title in November.

9/3—I am at the Jersey Shore for a few days to see my Mom while she is on her annual Labor Day week vacation. I forgot my power cord for my computer!! I can hardly do any work without it. It's all good though because it allowed me to relax and disconnect, which I needed. Everything happens for a reason, right? I know I just mentioned vacations last week but there's one more point I want to make.

⇨ Lesson #155: When you're on vacation, truly disconnect from work. Now THAT is a vacation and is super important, even if you're like me and love your job!

9/4—I took a nap today. I take naps often! They're much-needed sometimes. Studies vary on whether they are or aren't a good thing but certainly the Spanish like them, or we wouldn't all know about siestas! I do find that many times I sleep best at night when I do NOT take a nap during the day. However, if I didn't sleep enough the night before, then I definitely function better after a nap. If I don't rest, I am fighting to stay awake and not energized nor productive. (Funny side note: in writing this entry, I just let out a big yawn. Nap time!!)

⇨ Lesson #156: Listen to your body. If you are tired, take a nap. Obviously it's inconvenient in some situations—i.e. at work— but more and more companies are coming up with nap rooms, serenity rooms, etc. By the way, listening to your body is also relevant when you're not feeling well. Rest up, relax and if it's not better soon, go to the doctor.

9/5—This is one of my favorite times of year because the US Open tennis is on TV every day for two weeks. It provides so much fun and enjoyment in my life (and my Mom's too). We sat and watched, virtually nonstop, for the last three days. I am a huge fan of doing things that create greatness in multiple areas. For me, tuning in to "the Open" with my Mom helps me have fun and enjoyment but also family time. Win/win!

⇨ Lesson #157: Create win/win situations—fun and enjoyment with a family member, exercise with your significant other, a personal development workshop with your friends, etc.

9/6—Oh my! While I was at the Shore with my Mom, my new roommate Darnelle Radford straightened up and cleaned the entire apartment! Wow! I am beyond excited. Cleaning is one of my least favorite activities and due to my hectic schedule, even if I want to do it, I have little time to. I am grateful that a few days after he moved in, he took it upon himself to do this. While I'm at it, I also want to mention my prior roommate (Jim Hamilton) and thank him for two years and five months drama-free. Someone who cleans and someone who is drama free are the two things I like most about roommates!

9/7—Earlier this summer, to celebrate my success with the Life Coach Radio Networks, I made a rare expensive purchase. I treated myself to some prescription Burberry sunglasses. (I had a Groupon, so they were half off, but they were still . . . not cheap!) Anyway, within a month or two of buying them, I thought I lost them a few weeks ago. I hadn't been able to find them! Today I stumbled upon them tucked on a little shelf in my closet. I definitely don't remember putting them there but am excited to have them back. By the way, I wonder what else is in that messy closet!

⇨ Lesson #158: Use coupons, Groupons, shop at outlet malls, etc. Why pay full price when there are plenty of ways to save your hard-earned money?

9/8—Today, I am grateful for someone doing something he didn't have to do. The guy I lost badly to last weekend played with me just for fun and I played much better. Facing him helps me up my game. It's worth mentioning the lesson from April 4ᵗʰ again here. He "did something nice for someone". Here's another lesson:

⇨ Lesson #159: Think about how can you up your game—in sports and/or in life—and then go out and do it.

What did you learn from this week's entries and what changes can you make to live your best life?

_____

_____

_____

_____

9/9—I was out last night with one of my BFFs (Frenchy). He took a business card from the venue and wrote me a little note on the back of it that said "You make me happy". Isn't that nice? That, in turn, made me happy! I proudly displayed it on my dresser.

⇨ Lesson #160: When you get something that makes you happy, display it in your home as a reminder—for when you need it but also for when you don't.

9/10—Okay, I know I've posted a LOT about tennis lately. I promise this will be my last one for a while. I am grateful for Rafael Nadal and Novak Djokovic. They have an amazing rivalry as the top two players in men's game today. Watching them in the US Open final was thrilling! We're lucky to live in an era with them and Roger Federer and Andy Murray. From the French Open in 2005 through the US Open in 2013, that quartet has won the last 35 majors, except for the 2009 US Open, which was won by Juan Martin del Potro. Incredible!

9/11—Transformation is amazing. I see it so often in my clients during our sessions. Witnessing and/or being a part of that breakthrough is really neat. One woman was transformed tonight and many have been throughout the year so I thought it was finally worth mentioning.

9/12—I love Maya Angelou and value her insight. She often says she's grateful for everyday things—such as 'the light'. Isn't that a good one? We all take it for granted but on those days where maybe we can't think of something, it's an excellent go-to item. Nothing specific happened today to make me write about it, but I wanted to make sure I got it in somewhere in this book!

> ⇨ Lesson #161: If ever you're struggling to express gratitude on a certain day, choose things such as light, the sky, trees, air, breathing, etc. We take a lot for granted, and even someone who is struggling in life can be grateful for these things.

9/13—Last night, I got two nice notes—one from a client and another from a radio show host, both of whom thanked me for what I did. I know I've mentioned emails from others in prior posts in the book but I haven't yet said I'm grateful for gratitude, so here it is. I'm including their feedback not to pat myself on the back but to make sure everyone who reads this sees plenty of examples of what Life Coaching is. The client said:

"My original goal for today was to wrap up my LinkedIn profile. However that call was of huge value for me, thank you. You are very much helping me position my true value and aim myself in the right direction. The decision we came to about targeting around my best value reminds me of myself when I was 30 and single, very mobile, no family, and still young enough to take big risks. You helped me realize I am in that decision point once again and to stop limiting myself based upon perceived barriers."

The radio host said (after her debut) "it was SO much fun! Thanks for creating such a great avenue to share coaching, be with other coaches and a great place to market!"

9/14—I love when people pay me BEFORE the due date! (That happened today.)

> ⇨ Lesson #162: If you owe someone money (whether you borrowed it or you're doing business with them), consider paying them before it's due. They may need the money and may appreciate it immensely.

9/15—The miracle of childbirth is an amazing thing! Today I visited my friends Catherine and Brandon, who had a son a couple weeks ago. I've never seen a baby that young or small. It's incredibly neat. I just sat and stared at him while we lay on the bed.

What did you learn from this week's entries and what changes can you make to live your best life?

_____

_____

_____

_____

9/16—Cooler temperatures can come at the most opportune time! I had to wear a suit today, which is rare for me. I tend to perspire a bit and the early fall mildness outside is much appreciated!

9/17—Friends and loved ones supporting you on your projects is a wonderful thing. I saw my dear friend Amy Pawloski Dykie today. She always asks me a bunch of specific questions on how things are going. I always feel like she deeply cares. Amy says things such as "I'll tune into that. How can I listen to this?" I've mentioned support multiple times previously in the book as part of other posts but I want to make sure I highlight it here.

⇨ Lesson #163: How can you be supportive of the people in your life? This can mean donating to their fundraiser, verbal support, or anything really. Be like Amy and make sure you show how you feel via your actions.

9/18—These days, the roads seem to have more and more traffic on them. Drivers seem increasingly aggressive and just plain unsafe sometimes. For these reasons, I am now thankful every time I safely pull in my driveway! If you don't drive, there are other hazards out there. Not to be grim, but these include shootings, bombings and severe weather.

⇨ Lesson #164: Be glad and/or relieved every time you arrive home safely. It gives you something to be grateful for every day, even if you take public transit or walk!

9/19—Abundance is great, especially as an entrepreneur. Today, I appeared in someone's blog. Tomorrow, I am going to be on someone's radio show and then leading an online workshop (that the company is paying me for—they found me!) Thank you!

9/20—A while ago, I got selected to give a keynote speech at Bentley University for the Alpha Kappa Psi Northeast Region Leadership Retreat. It's tomorrow in Boston. I'm SO excited. (And this is rare, but just a little nervous). I'm honored and humbled to have been chosen and am working super hard today to figure out what I want to say, how I want to say it, while also keeping it conversational and knowing my talking points well enough so I don't have to look at my notes.

9/21—The keynote speech went AMAZING today. I am very happy with it and received great feedback from those in attendance. I practiced a lot, which definitely paid off.

⇨ Lesson #165: Talk to yourself when practicing speeches. Be conversational! Whatever you do in the actual speech, don't read from a piece of paper! Simply have a few notes but speak from the heart and trust the words will come.

9/22—Chances are, if you're reading this book, water is something you can be grateful for. There are many health benefits of drinking a lot of water. Many people around the world don't have access to clean water. I talk a lot and often need some to keep my mouth lubricated. It's especially relevant today because I was talking a lot at the conference yesterday.

⇨ Lesson #166: Drink 64 ounces of water a day. Many health experts say eight 8 oz. glasses. I personally drink six 11oz. glasses. However you do it, just figure out a way to do it. Even Oprah strives to drink more water!

What did you learn from this week's entries and what changes can you make to live your best life?

_____

_____

_____

_____

9/23—I had some time to reflect today on my speech from the weekend and want to share the key points with you. Earlier in the book I referenced the Platinum rule (do unto others as they want done unto them, not as you would do unto yourself). That's always my top tip when discussing Leadership. The other things I shared in Boston include understanding the difference between introverts and extroverts, giving feedback timely, and seeking feedback from team members on how the department and/or organization can function better. I am also a firm believer in "keeping it real" when giving feedback. If someone is off the charts excellent, don't come up with a negative just to have something constructive. On the flip side, if someone is a poor performer, don't waste their time and yours trying to think of the one positive thing they do well.

⇨ Lesson #167: If you're a Leader, assess how you are performing in these areas. If you're not yet a Leader, file this lesson/advice away in a place you will remember for when you become one!

9/24—I love when people are proactive. In the last few days, I've gotten a number of emails, Twitter interactions and other social media posts from participants in the aforementioned workshop. I didn't get to speak to some of them one-on-one. I'm glad they have reached out since then, so we can start to develop a relationship. I am SO impressed with today's youth. Their commitment to service is inspiring, as is their unbridled enthusiasm and the fact that they know a lot of things those of us from older generations don't.

⇨ Lesson #168: Make sure you have some current college students—or at least some people in their twenties—in your network. You'll learn and be inspired!

9/25—I ran into a long lost pal on the train tonight. It's such a fun random thing. He moved away a few years ago and I didn't even know he was back in town. It was energizing seeing him and catching up on all that's happened in our lives in recent years.

9/26—I love when the memory of something makes me laugh. I was buying some new sneakers today and, whenever I am buying shoes, I remember this time as a kid when we were at the shoe store. My Mom was trying to help my sister into some sneakers and kept saying "Stop curling your toes!" because April's foot wouldn't go in. As it turns out, my sister wasn't curling her toes. There was one of those balls of paper in the shoe and THAT'S why she couldn't get the shoe on! (My awesome Mom gave me her blessing for sharing this story!)

9/27—Movies are a great activity for friends, dates or by yourself. They're easy to enjoy with minimal planning and it's exciting to go on opening night. My pal Craig Washington and I went this evening and had fun. We had been looking forward to it for a while. The movie wasn't the best but that wasn't the point. The camaraderie between two best buds was!

Tonight reminded me of an outing during my frequent volunteering with Big Brothers Big Sisters. A few years ago, I took one of my Little Brothers to the movies and he was really excited about it. Many of us take going to the movies for granted. He and his family couldn't afford to go, so it was quite a treat for him. It was a special moment in my life being able to witness (and be a part of) his excitement.

⇨ Lesson #169: Appreciate things you commonly treat yourself to (such as movies, dinners out, etc.) that those who are not as fortunate may not get to experience.

9/28—Today in NYC I was lucky to attend (for free) the Global Citizens Festival concert. It's an event to raise awareness, celebrate success and accelerate progress to a world without extreme poverty by 2030. Oh my word what an experience it was. The performances by many of the stars were incredible, but the legendary Stevie Wonder was out of this world. I had never seen him before and LOVE his music. He's incredibly talented and is an excellent example of my next lesson . . .

> ⇨ Lesson #170: Don't let things stop you! Stevie Wonder is blind but uses his other talents to the fullest. Instead of dwelling on whatever disabilities or perceived shortcomings you have, use your energy to figure out how to be happy and successful despite those things.

9/29—I appreciate new recipes, especially when they allow me to experience delicious food in a new way AND they're easy, which is what I need for my busy life. My Mom shared one with me today (chicken parmesan and pasta in the crock pot). I tried it tonight and it was yummy! I envision myself making this a lot.

What did you learn from this week's entries and what changes can you make to live your best life?

_____

_____

_____

_____

9/30—Have you tried bartering? It's great! You help someone and they help you in return. I met someone via LinkedIn who is interested in becoming a Life Coach. I've been mentoring her, explaining what is necessary to change to this great career, how it's been for me, etc. Somehow we got to talking and I mentioned in passing that I'm way behind on my bookkeeping. She said "Oh I love doing that stuff!" We agreed to trade my coaching her for her updating my income spreadsheets. What a great arrangement! I am incredibly thankful for her help!!

⇨ Lesson #171: Does bartering appeal to you? If so, what situations can you create for yourself where you can swap something you're good at and enjoy for something you don't like (or don't have time for) that someone else does?

10/1—I found out today that a client lost 25 pounds after just two sessions with me! I love when people are INSPIRED to ACTION as a result of our INTERACTION.

10/2—Today, I am grateful for sharing—online and in life. One of my coaches—Tim Billiter, who I am also proud to call a friend—shared one of my YouTube videos on Facebook this evening. I'm thankful because now a lot more people have seen it. Also, I've written already about knowledge sharing but there are plenty of other things you can share: your time, something delicious you cooked or baked, or even a personal story that may make someone feel better.

⇨ Lesson #172: Make it a point to share more—whether it's something tangible or intangible.

10/3—Being spontaneous is liberating! My schedule is super crazy and I don't always have the luxury of doing it, but this week my dear friend Elaine Green and I decided to drive up to see our alma mater (Syracuse University) honor our favorite actor (Taye Diggs) with a distinguished alumni award. It was a bit hectic making the trip happen. (I spent ten hours in the car and 14 hours in Syracuse.) It was well worth it though. We had great quality time together and got to snap a picture with Taye before he had to go backstage.

⇨ Lesson #173: Wouldn't it be funny if I told you to plan to be spontaneous? Seriously though, when the opportunity to "live a little more than you normally would" knocks on your door, pull the door open and figure out how you can let spontaneity in.

10/4—On our road trip, Elaine split the driving with me. Hooray! Most long car rides I am by myself and have to do it all. I am thankful she was with me. I was tired going up and coming back. I'm yawning just thinking about it!

10/5—One last post on my trip to my old stomping grounds . . . colleges and universities are wonderful! Learning is amazing and I feel even more energized than normal by being in that inspiring environment again. I'm happy I carved out time to go.

⇨ Lesson #174: Figure out a way to visit your alma mater sometime soon. Interact with current students. See what changes (aesthetically and otherwise) have happened. I promise you'll be glad you went!

10/6—Public parks are great. It's lovely to experience them for free. Today, I met a client in one park and gave a tennis lesson in another. The park closest to me in Jersey City has a cool fountain for kids that my niece and nephew loved when they visited. Even in a city, there are plenty of pockets of nature for you to enjoy.

⇨ Lesson #175: if you haven't fully explored and/or utilized the parks near you, give them a try.

What did you learn from this week's entries and what changes can you make to live your best life?

_____

_____

_____

_____

10/7—Today, I was talking with a fellow Coach (Laura Rivchun), whom I just met a couple weeks ago, and she said "You're very genuine". I pride myself on this. I think it's one of the highest compliments you can give someone. To be seen as authentic and sincere and not hypocritical, nor pretentious, is a great feeling.

⇨ Lesson #176: How do you want to be seen by others? Take a moment to ponder the characteristics you value, and then think if your daily actions are reflective of these traits.

10/8—My awesome Mom turned 70 today. I am so proud of her. She is thriving in retirement, living her best life, enjoying time with friends, playing tennis three times a week, seeing her grandkids often, and simply continuing to be the great lady that she is. We had a lovely day celebrating: my sister April, my Aunt Dolly (who is still going strong at 82 by the way) and I took my Mom out to breakfast and then to one of her favorite activities—the casino! It was wonderful that the four of us were able to spend the majority of the day together. In the evening, I joined April, my brother-in-law John and their kids in taking my Mom out to dinner, which also was a fun experience. I know she had a great day.

⇨ Lesson #177: What special activities can you do on your birthday or a loved one's birthday to ensure, at the very least, on that day during the year, you spend a lot of quality time together?

10/9—This morning I was walking up the stairs from my sister's basement and saw green trees and blue sky outside her sliding glass door. It was a beautiful, peaceful sight. I have a great view of the sky and a nice old church out of my bedroom window at home, but there was something about this spectacle this morning that was extra special. Maybe rising up from below (i.e. the basement) had something to do with it.

⇨ Lesson #178: You may have noticed that even though the view at my sister's was spectacular, I am still grateful for what I have (the view at my home).

10/10—I love getting positive feedback! Isn't it great? I am working part-time as a Publicist for someone and she said "have I told you how blessed I feel to have you working on my behalf? It was the perfect solution for me at the right time." This totally made my day!

⇨ Lesson #179: Consider who you can give positive feedback to today, and go out and do it.

10/11—Have you been to a reunion lately? They are so fun, whether it's something formal for your high school or college, or an informal gathering of friends. This weekend the aforementioned Karen Collins was back in NYC for the first time since her move to Seattle a few months ago. A group of our fellow Life Coach friends gathered to catch up with her but also each other. Life is so busy at times that, even when people are all in the same city, it's hard carving out the time to meet up.

⇨ Lesson #180: Are you cultivating your social relationships? What friend(s) haven't you seen or talked to in a while? Reach out to them and find out what's up and/or make a plan to meet.

10/12—They paved the road I live by and travel on often! First, I love the smell of fresh asphalt LOL. Second, I am grateful because it had a lot of potholes and now the ride on it is much more pleasant.

10/13—I went to a delightful wedding today and witnessed my friends Jenni Lewis and Levon Ford get married. There are many things to love about an experience such as this but being invited is at the top of my list. It's an honor and a privilege to be a witness to their love on their big day. I've had two weddings in the last two months. One was for one of my first NYC friends (Elaine Green), who I've known longer than almost everyone else here—13.5 years. As for Levon Ford and Jenni Lewis-Ford, I just met them last year. I'm glad I'm already close enough to them that I was invited to the wedding. Another thing I love about weddings is how fun they are! The DJ was great at both weddings and their friends and family and I danced and danced, seemingly all night. The third great thing about weddings is the food! Oh my word, I ate so much. I always enjoy eating food I don't normally prepare at home.

What did you learn from this week's entries and what changes can you make to live your best life?

_____

_____

_____

_____

10/14—I am grateful for GPS. I missed my turn on my trip from where the wedding was (in upstate NY) to Montreal and didn't realize it for quite a few exits UGH! Instead of having to backtrack, at least it was able to help me cut across. I've actually gotten lost four times in the last three days! I like to think I excel in many areas, but navigation is definitely not one of them! Anyway, thank goodness for GPS and its ability to help me find my way. It's SO convenient. How did we live without it?

10/15—This evening, Joachim and I went to a cool 24 hour outdoor Produce market in Montreal. I love going to them and frequent my local one in Jersey City often. The prices are often much cheaper than the big supermarkets and shopping at them helps me accomplish this next lesson.

⇨ Lesson #181: Support local businesses! This is one of my many missions or goals in life. Not only does it likely help the owners make a living, but I personally find it a more pleasant shopping experience. The retail establishment is often much smaller, and therefore you don't have to park far away and/or walk the equivalent of a few city blocks between aisles.

10/16—The leaves are starting to turn! I witnessed some beautiful fall foliage today. There were lovely views in the Adirondacks on my way home from seeing Joachim. I swear this is one of the most picturesque places I have ever seen. It is lovely in the winter and the fall. I will have to notice what it is like in the other seasons.

10/17—Tonight, the Life Coach Radio Networks team had a planning call for our first ever Workshop Weekend. It's going to be a big event where 10-15 of us come together to give workshops, panel discussions, etc. I had the idea a while ago but didn't think we could make it happen already (which is rare for me—I usually am in 'GO FOR IT' mode). But on our last call a few weeks ago, one of my colleagues suggested it and many hosts raised their hand to help! Not only is it moving forward now, but best of all, the team is planning it! I don't have to lift a finger!!

⇨ Lesson #182: You don't have to do everything yourself. Often, bringing smart people together is enough. Relinquish control and empower others!

10/18—Tonight is the big celiac disease fundraiser that Danielle Mund and I have been planning for months. We are so excited. It's been a busy last few weeks preparing for it and I am glad all things seem to be in order and we're good to go. I am grateful to everyone who donated (individuals and also companies donating their products). She and I have worked tirelessly on this. It's been excellent being involved in this project with her. Her dedication is off the charts amazing.

10/19—The fundraiser last night was a huge success. Not only did we raise more than $9,000 for the University of Chicago Celiac Disease Center, but the event was super fun! As I termed it, we put the FUN in FUNDRAISER. We received a lot of great feedback from people who said they really enjoyed themselves, wanted to find out about the next event, etc. I'm excited by and proud of all we accomplished. We had the idea on May 31 and decided to "do it" in mid-June. To go from idea to "game day" in just four months is impressive. I won't lie there were a few doubts along the way, but either Danielle or I just reassured the other that "this WILL happen and WILL be amazingly successful."

⇨ Lesson #183: Don't give up. Never give up! Making something big happen will take time and determination. Once you lock in the former, always remember the latter is under your control.

By the way, if you want to support the cause, go to: http://www.cureceliacdisease.org/donate-now. Thank you!

10/20—I love the feeling of taking my socks and shoes off at the end of a long day. Ahhhhhh. Can you feel my relief coming through the pages?

What did you learn from this week's entries and what changes can you make to live your best life?

_____

_____

_____

_____

10/21—Having a Plan B is a great thing. Back in the spring, my pal Ben Moon and I wanted to play tennis and my main park that I go to was closed to the public because the high school teams were on the courts. Luckily, Ben knew about a little hidden park with two courts, so we went there. I was able to use that spot again today with my friend (and Championship match opponent) Kristof Goeser. I'm glad I know about it and that Ben shared this gem with me. By the way, sometimes in life, a Plan B can turn out far better than your first option. Back when I was contemplating leaving my corporate job to become a Life Coach, I was trying to find another job but nothing worked out, so, I made the leap to become an entrepreneur. I had no idea at the time that I would love it so much—much more than working for a big firm (or anyone for that matter).

⇨ Lesson #184: Don't be afraid to have a plan B. It could turn out to be amazing. I give my plan B an A++!

10/22—Aren't hugs lovely? I got a great one today at lunch from my friend and former colleague Lu Ann Vispoli. I always tell her she gives the best hugs. I can literally and figuratively feel the love when she does it.

⇨ Lesson #185: When appropriate, hug someone like you really mean it. We hug people often but at times we probably do it half-heartedly.

10/23—Here's to being popular. I don't mean it from a standpoint of "Who's popular in high school", which often has a negative connotation. I got a nice email today from my contact at the nonprofit agency where I've given a LinkedIn workshop a couple times in recent months. She said that it's become their "most popular" one. This is excellent. It means that the insights I have to share and the topics I cover are resonating with a lot of people. I'm glad that I'm having a positive impact on the attendees' lives. Incidentally, I facilitate the workshops for free at this organization, so here is the next lesson:

⇨ Lesson #186: Consider donating your time, wisdom, etc. to your favorite local nonprofit. I bet the people there will not only appreciate it but also benefit from it.

10/24—I've mentioned written cards before but today I want to highlight written thank you notes! I got two this week, one from my Mom and another from my friend Catherine, both with appreciation for the recent birthday and baby gifts, respectively.

⇨ Lesson #187: Don't forget the written thank you note. It's a lost art but often it's much appreciated by the recipient.

10/25—I must admit I love TV. When I retire, my main goals are going to be to socialize, exercise and watch television. My parents used to joke that they wondered if I would get couch sores from watching so much TV! These days though, my time is much more limited. The only time I do it is when eating meals at home. However, in those short nuggets of time, I spent this week catching up on last season of *The Good Wife*. I've also recently got into *Scandal*. Both shows are excellent and a nice (and much-needed) respite from my busy life these days.

⇨ Lesson #188: Even if you have a super busy life, make time for fun and enjoyment. I can't say enough how important it is to have balance and not work too much.

10/26—Today, I was at the mall making some purchases for myself and while I was in line I saw a lovely charm bracelet that I think my Mom will love. I'm not a big fan of Christmas shopping—although I love giving gifts—so the fact that this appeared made my day and will make things easier on December 24th, which is usually the day I start my shopping! (By the way, the message on the box said "Mom, you are the heart of the family". I could not agree more.)

10/27—Being caught up is a wonderful feeling! I've had a lot of work to do this week and have been behind but tonight I finished the major stuff that was hanging over my head. The phrase Playing Catchup is ironic because when I appeared on *Wheel of Fortune* in 2012, that was one of the puzzles and I did NOT solve it! I wanted to say "Oh my god I do that all the time how did I not get it?!" I did solve four others though and won "five figures" in cash and prizes. It was SUCH an awesome experience! If you want to see highlights of the episode, I have video clips on my Facebook. See the epilogue for how to connect with me on it and other forms of social media.

What did you learn from this week's entries and what changes can you make to live your best life?

_____

_____

_____

_____

10/28—Today, I am grateful for waking up, having to use the bathroom really badly and my roommate NOT being in there! It seems simple but we've all probably been in those situations where we had "to go" and it was being used by someone else. I'm glad that wasn't the case today.

10/29—This afternoon on the highway, a car swerved into my lane. I am glad no one was in the next lane because I had to swerve into it to avoid being hit. The roads are more and more dangerous due to phone calls, texting and otherwise distracted drivers.

⇨ Lesson #189: When driving, know where other cars are and anticipate things that could go wrong so that you are fully prepared if they do.

10/30—I almost forgot an important appointment today. I am glad that I have everything listed in my Google calendar and that I saw it this morning. I promptly set my alarm for it to make sure I am free and ready for this phone call.

10/31—Happy Halloween! It's such a fun holiday for kids to go around in their costumes and for grown-ups to gather, see friends and party, which was exactly what I did this evening!

11/1—It's great to see new businesses popping up. I was with my BFF Gen Caruncho (in town from Miami) and, after we had lunch with her boyfriend in a crowded restaurant, he had to go back to the hotel and do work, so she and I decided to go somewhere for dessert. Practically right across the street from the restaurant was this cute new ice cream and baked goods place. It was spacious (rare in NYC), quiet, and the treats were delicious and not too overpriced. We spent another hour together chatting about all kinds of things and catching up on life. So lovely!

11/2—I know that climate change may be a factor, but there was unseasonably warm weather today and I was able to play tennis outside! It was sunny and in the 60s in NYC in early November, which is quite rare.

11/3—Today I had the privilege of watching five of my friends—Lora Boltniew, Joy Tegtmeyer, Achilles Yeldell, Luis Nunez and Stacey

Dettling—run in and complete the NYC Marathon. I have a favorite, not-too-crowded spot in Queens that I go to that makes it easy for the runners to spot me. I saw all five of them and they stopped, we hugged and posed for a picture, chatted briefly, and then they got back to their 26.2 miles. Their dedication is nothing short of amazing. The time they put in, the pain they go through, the fundraising they do—all incredible and I'm proud and honored to call them my friends. In addition to them, I saw THOUSANDS of others. I cheered them on too like I had known them for years. It's inspiring to see all the different runners—old or disabled, young and healthy, skinny and not skinny, and everyone in between.

⇨ Lesson #190: Find out where the closest marathon is to you and plan to see it. I promise you'll be glad you did. It's free inspiration. Who doesn't want that?

What did you learn from this week's entries and what changes can you make to live your best life?

_____

_____

_____

_____

11/4—Two years ago today, I found out I was cancer free. I didn't actually have cancer, but I went through a period of days and weeks of being worried sick after my Ear, Nose and Throat doctor told me she thought I may have lymphoma. I had to go to multiple appointments at one of the cancer hospitals here in NYC. It was upsetting—lots of anxiety, waiting for results, etc. I tried to be strong and not tell my family until everything was OK. That lasted about one minute. As soon as my Mom saw me during that period, she knew right away that something was wrong. (As she says, Mom-ism #3, "a Mother knows".) I am grateful I am not just alive, but thriving. I am also very thankful to my BFF Anika Johnson and my brother-in-law John Reavy for each taking a turn going with me to my doctor appointments. It was great to have their moral support and I really appreciate them taking a full day out of their busy "parents of young kids" schedule to be by my side when I needed them.

⇨ Lesson #191: Get your annual physical. Many people do it around their birthday because it's an easy way to remember it.

⇨ Lesson #192: If your primary care doctor recommends that you see a specialist for something, do it! Yes it involves extra time, appointments, etc., but with your health it's better to be safe than sorry.

11/5—Role models are an excellent thing. Married couple Andrea and Taharqa Patterson sang "You've Got a Friend" as the big finale last night at Toshi's. They're a great example of love and marrying your best friend. It was inspiring to see. Not only are they super talented singers, but the friendship and love between them as they sang was visible and palpable.

⇨ Lesson #193: Ask yourself who your role models are. I'm envisioning everyday people who you can establish and/or cultivate a relationship with. Spend time with these people and learn from their experience.

11/6—This afternoon I am grateful for lunch with my friend Katie Fabian. First of all, it's always great to reconnect with a former colleague and make plans for more frequent interactions. (Before I became self-employed, she and I sat two rows away from each other in our little cubicles and we went to lunch once a month, chatted at the water cooler or in the hallway, etc. I miss that, but nothing else about my former job LOL!) Secondly, as someone who works from home now, many days I eat breakfast, lunch and dinner in my condo. As you can imagine, that can be a bit monotonous, even if I am a great cook. I was excited not just to see her but to have a great reason to go out and eat some different food!

11/7—Today I found out a friend's mother died (Delores Lee, to whom this book is dedicated. She's the mother of Ken Lee and mother-in-law to Ayanna Lee, who is one of my BFFs.) I am glad I got to speak to Mr. Lee yesterday to let them know I was thinking of them. This was my second friend's Mom to pass away in the last month or two. Both women were in their 60s and died soon after finding out they were sick with cancer. It's sad. I can't even imagine what the families are going through. I feel lucky and fortunate that I've never had to experience something like that. Death sucks.

⇨ Lesson #194: Please live every day to the fullest, okay?

11/8—I've talked a lot about mentoring in this book but haven't yet said how grateful I am for MY mentors, who I am also honored and proud to call my friends. This week it's especially relevant because I've interacted with three of them recently. First, let me thank Cheyenne Bostick (also known as Ask Chey B) for agreeing to do the foreword for my book. I spoke to my publishers today and they said I need one. I reached out to him and he replied/said yes within a few hours. I can't wait to see what he writes. I also want to mention Dawn Doherty, a super successful coach who is excited about doing workshops and webinars with ME! Finally, I had lunch with Karen Sullivan and she gave me some great advice for doing more Life Coach Training at the school we graduated from (and both teach at). My favorite mentoring advice is to pull people up, which I mentioned back on May 9th. This happened to me when I was in corporate too. Many times we have to work SO hard to get promoted or to get additional opportunities. It's wonderful when someone taps us on the shoulder and says "I choose you". Choose someone. Pull them up.

11/9—Today I received the "Cy Young" award as best pitcher in my softball division this past summer. (I had six wins and no losses in helping my team to a 10-6 record and second place.) I got a cool medal and they called me up on stage at the season ending party. It's always great to get recognition on a job well done.

⇨ Lesson #195: I've written about positive feedback before but I want to highlight something slightly different here. Give recognition to people who work for you (or with you) or who are otherwise in your life. It can be something formal—a tangible token of your appreciation—or even just a verbal "I want to recognize you for the excellent job you did . . ."

11/10—This may sound simple but I am glad I don't get as many emails on the weekends, when most people are busy enjoying time with their family and friends. I, on the other hand, am working but that's totally fine because I love what I do and what I am building— and I make time for socializing throughout the week. I get a lot done on weekends and am less behind on my sea of emails and social media notifications.

What did you learn from this week's entries and what changes can you make to live your best life?

_____

_____

_____

_____

11/11—Two years ago today—on 11/11/11—I got a really bad performance evaluation from my then boss. After some time reflecting, I soon decided to leave that situation but didn't know what I wanted to do next. As I mentioned back in a July entry, within a span of a few weeks, Lora Boltniew and Tamarra Causley Robinson, who didn't know each other, said "Have you ever thought about being a Life Coach?" After not one but TWO signs from God, the rest as they say is HIStory! I love my new path and am happy I had that bad experience, because it led to this. Some people in my situation would still be bitter or angry at their former boss for causing so much grief and stress. I'm actually grateful for him.

⇨ Lesson #196: Know that everything happens for a reason. This boss was brought into my life so that I would be on this incredible path I am on now!

11/12—Yesterday was Mrs. Lee's funeral. It was the most beautiful and uplifting funeral I've ever been to and I'm thankful I was there to experience it. There is and was so much love for her in Calvary Baptist Church and beyond. Many people gave eulogies and talked about how devoted she was to kids. I witnessed this firsthand. Three months ago yesterday, I was standing in her kitchen at the luncheon she hosted after the christening for Ken and Ayanna's daughter Katie. Mrs. Lee was telling a couple guests that I was on *Wheel of Fortune* last year. We all talked about it and I pulled up the videos. It was fun. Later I was standing in the foyer and found out that these guests were kids that she and her husband took in many years ago when they had nowhere else to go. I assumed they were family members, but then after thinking about it some more, I realized that they were. All kids were Mrs. Lee's family.

That day, I had no idea she was sick. She seemed her enthusiastic, great hostess self, with her trademark hearty laugh. I admire how she dealt with her illness. She didn't tell people. She wanted them to treat her with the same love, respect and fun vibe that they normally did, not to have pity on her for what was soon going to happen. She truly lived every last day to the fullest. When someone dies, their body isn't here with us anymore but their soul lives on forever. I know I will always be touched by Mrs. Lee's soul.

⇨ Lesson #197: When a loved one passes away, as the sadness starts to fade, think about what you can learn from their life and use it to improve the quality of your own life. You only get one.

I hope these entries about her inspire even one person to change his/her path. If so, then I'm helping Mrs. Lee's legacy live on.

11/13—In need of some fun after an emotional start to the week, I met superstar Ricky Martin last night! He had a book signing for his recently-published kids book *Santiago the Dreamer in Land Among the Stars*. It's about a young performer who learns to overcome rejection and follow his dreams. I must admit I went to the event because it was Ricky Martin (hello!) but I am happy that his book fits perfectly with the change I am trying to see happen in the world.

⇨ Lesson #198: Go for your dreams! Don't let rejection stop you. One of my wise clients (Greg Pilla) heard advice recently to strive for a lot of NOs. The more you get, the better your chances for some YESs.

By the way, I also must add how great Ricky seems—yes I am on a first name basis with him now! I've been to a lot of events with celebrities and I think he holds the record for the longest period of time and enthusiasm! He must have signed for at least two hours. There had to be more than 1,000 people there. He conversed with and/ or took pictures with *every* one of us. Here was our brief exchange:

Me: "Hi Ricky!! I was born in 1971 too."
Ricky: "Oh really? Cool, man. They say we are from the year of the pig."
Scintillating right?? LOL

11/14—I am a huge fan of people being inclusive, in all aspects of life and work. (I worked for two years as a Diversity champion, so it's something I'm passionate about.) Anyway, last night my super talented pal Kevin Thompson performed in a sketch comedy show. I hadn't seen him in YEARS. I waited outside the theatre door for him after his hilarious show. (His imitation of Olivia Pope from *Scandal* was so funny.) I would have been happy to say "Hey Kevin, great show, way to go, how are you? See you soon" but he insisted that I come with him, the cast and his other friends, who were all going to a bar and restaurant down the street. I was flattered and honored. He's an up and coming star with some national TV appearances and is already at the maximum of 5,000 Facebook friends (a sure sign of soon-to-be big success in my mind). Also, he and I have never 'broken bread' together, which as you may recall is one of the things I treasure—when a friendship reaches that level. As I mentioned before, my goal as a Life Coach is to get people from Functional to Optimal. Seeing Kevin and chatting for a few minutes would have been functional. By him inviting me out and me having a great time with him and his other friends, he created an optimal situation for me. I had much more fun than I otherwise would have. I'm grateful for him. He's a great role model for his infant son.

⇨ Lesson #199: Be inclusive. Think of situations where you can invite someone to something, or have them participate in an initiative or project (if work-related) that will help them have a more optimal life.

11/15—I noticed that the loud crossing guard (who I have frequently been awakened by) at the intersection outside my window has been replaced by a quiet one. I never caught her name (usually because I was always trying to go back to sleep whenever she was around) but hopefully all is well with her and she's . . . how can I say this politely . . . still going strong and waking someone else up instead. Or even better maybe she's by a high rise where the windows aren't a few feet from her. I am glad I can sleep a little better now.

11/16—Feeling a sense of accomplishment is an amazing thing. Today I had my book editors over for a big group review together. I had SO much catching up to do prior to them coming. I basically had to write for at least 90 minutes a day every day for the last week. (My process in writing this book is to identify 'the thing' for each day as it happens but then to go back and write the paragraph when I have large chunks of time—on flights, etc. That hadn't happened since August, which is how behind I was!) Anyway, I busted my behind this week to make sure everything was done and ready for them. I can't tell you how good I felt that I got everything done.

11/17—I won the tennis Championship last night. Thirty-four matches played and only two losses. I want to thank my opponent and friend Kristof Goeser for being gracious in defeat. Also kudos to my practice partner Phillip Pegues. Finally thanks to my friend Stacey Moyers, who gave me an energy bar when I saw her recently. I don't usually eat them so I saved it for my match. I scarfed it down during the second set when I needed to come back from a 3-1 deficit.

What did you learn from this week's entries and what changes can you make to live your best life?

_____

_____

_____

_____

11/18—Today I am grateful for forgiveness. This weekend I did something that, in hindsight, I wish I hadn't. A few years ago, after I made a mistake that I was upset about, my friend Shaun James told me, "You know what your problem is Russ? You're human. We make mistakes." That wise advice while we were sitting in the car has stayed with me. Anyway, back to this weekend, I was again upset at my actions and, for the last couple days, was worried that my BFF who was with me at the time (Frenchy) was also upset. He was that night, momentarily, but then, as I found out today, he quickly forgave me. I feel incredibly relieved.

⇨ Lesson #200: Forgiveness is a great virtue to have. Are you blessed with it? Do you use it? Staying mad and holding on to resentment hurts you primarily—not the other person. Try not to be angry for long. Letting the anger go will set you free. Get ready to soar!

11/19—I'm hosting my big annual pre-Thanksgiving dinner party this weekend. It's going to be a hectic week because I'm away for a few days and at Rutgers University all day Friday. I ran to the supermarket today to buy everything I needed for Saturday's meal and all the sale and other items were in stock! This is actually a little bit rare. The grocery store that I go to the most is "sometimes-to-usually" out of at least one thing on my list. Not today though . . . thank goodness!

11/20—This week, I am spending time in The Hamptons with my friend, mentor and colleague Dawn Doherty. She and her husband Bob recently purchased a beautiful home there and invited me to visit.

Their house is magnificent!! Wow! The area is very nice too. I had never been there before and had been looking forward to this trip for weeks. I always enjoy having something nice to look forward to.

> ⇨ Lesson #201: Make sure you often have an exciting thing in your future. The anticipation will get you through any rough patches or down days.

I am a firm believer in sharing the wealth. Dawn and Bob didn't have to invite me to come, especially so soon after they moved in. Recently, I've experienced other examples of people doing this. My coach Lisa Giuliano, who I affectionately call Judy LOL, treats me to lunch more often than I treat her. Comedian Chelsea Handler and Oprah were talking on TV earlier this year about treating their friends and their theory is, if someone makes a good deal more money than the other, he/she should pay for his/her friends when out to eat. I'm not saying go out and do this on every occasion but . . .

> ⇨ Lesson #202: If you're in a situation where you can 'share the wealth', consider doing it. I bet the person will appreciate you sharing your good fortune. If Lisa buys me lunch, and I buy my Little Brother (through Big Brothers Big Sisters) Russell Short dinner, and he buys his younger cousin something from the corner store, just think of all that goodwill and all those good feelings we've created!

11/21—While at Dawn's, I sat in the most comfortable desk chair. Wow! In my home, I usually work on the couch, which is certainly comfy in its own way. I am grateful for the nice lower back support and proper form that her chair provided.

11/22—To me, there are few things better than having leftovers in the refrigerator after a long drive home. I was hungry after my trip back from The Hamptons last night and had one of those "warm up dinner late and then off to bed" nights. It was the perfect end to a great trip.

11/23—Tonight is my 8ᵗʰ annual pre-Thanksgiving dinner, a potluck affair held every year the weekend before Thanksgiving. It allows my friends and me to gather as if we were family (and in many cases, friends are family) before some people head their separate ways for the Holiday. Especially here in NYC, not everyone has an opportunity to return home to see their family. This dinner helps make sure people experience that feeling of togetherness, whether they go back to their hometown later in the week or not.

⇨ Lesson #203: I wrote in a prior lesson about being aware of your friends. Around the holidays, be extra aware of the people in your life. It's a rough time for many, especially those who are lonely/alone, experienced a recent loss of a loved one, not close to family (figuratively and/or literally), etc. Do what you can to open your home to them, if only for a dinner.

11/24—Last night's party was a fantastic time! I love a lot of things about having people over—the camaraderie, the catching up, the laughs, friends meeting other friends, etc. One thing I do to record this moment in my history is to ask people to sign a guest book before they leave. (It's an idea I got from Oprah MANY years ago.) I ask them to write a few lines about their experience while they were here. Reading it always puts a huge smile on my face. I often flip through the guest book and see what people wrote years ago. I'm grateful for fun memories and being able to relive these happy experiences years later.

⇨ Lesson #204: Consider having a guest book in your home. I promise you will be glad you did.

What did you learn from this week's entries and what changes can you make to live your best life?

_____

_____

_____

_____

11/25—There is a new crossing signal at the busy intersection at the end of my street. I am excited. I must cross here every time I take the train. It used to just say "Walk" or "Don't Walk" but now it gives you the seconds you have left before the light changes. This is such an upgrade and keeps us safer!

11/26—Here is a "keeping it real" moment for you. Today, I had to use a public bathroom and it had just been cleaned. Let me tell you it was quite lovely!! The toilets still had blue water and the entire rest room smelled nice! Personally, I love it when this happens. It is quite rare and often we experience the other extreme, which is less than pleasant.

11/27—You may recall my entry from early May, when I made my flight by the skin of my teeth, somehow getting from my living room in Jersey City onto the plane in Newark in 55 minutes. Today, it was a train I just barely caught! Here's the scenario: the train I usually take comes on the 9s (for example, 10:09, 10:19, etc.). Usually I leave my living room no later than the 2 and I am on it by the 7 (or the 8 at the latest because sometimes it leaves early). Anyway, today I left on the 3 (talk about living life on the edge) AND got stopped at the aforementioned light. I power-walked the rest of the way, except for running from the bottom of the stairs through the train doors just as they were closing and keeping me on time for my meeting in NYC. Phew!

11/28—Today is Thanksgiving, the best day of the year to be grateful! My mom makes everyone go around the dinner table and say what they're thankful for. This is such an excellent exercise.

> ⇨ Lesson #205: Encourage those around you to practice gratitude—at a minimum on Thanksgiving and at a maximum . . . more than that! Perhaps a good compromise between once a year and daily is every holiday, or once a week. You can do it with them and can decide together on timing. Activities are fun and enriching when we take part in them with others.

My gas tank was practically on empty today, I'm thankful that the gas station I usually go to was open. I tried to be extra nice to the attendant. I appreciate all the people who work on holidays so that the rest of us can get to our destination, buy last minute groceries, go out to dinner, etc.

11/29—Tonight, I was tired after a long day and didn't feel like going out. Two friends contacted me and said "We were thinking of stopping over is that OK?" It was not only OK, it was perfect!!

11/30—One of my new favorite things is Meetup.com, which "helps groups of people with shared interests plan meetings and form offline clubs in local communities around the world." (That definition is off its website and is way better than I could have done describing it!) My BFF Anika Johnson suggested to her fiancé (and my friend) Mike Washington that he look into it for football games in our area. He did and found a great group of guys practically down the street from them. I had wanted to play with them too and was not able to attend the last few weeks. I was finally able to go today and it was so much fun. The other players were exactly as Mike said—nice and fun to play with. I intend to play with them almost every Saturday until softball season starts in April!

⇨ Lesson #206: If you are looking to meet people in any area, meetup.com is a great way to do it. The opportunities are endless—business and entrepreneurial, self-improvement, social, sports, etc.

12/1—Today, I saw the phrase Positive Mental Attitude and had a flashback to about 25 years ago. I totally forgot about it but my Mom used to say this all the time when we played mixed doubles tennis together (which was often). We actually won a tournament as a team, which was super fun at the time and makes me happy and proud looking back on it. Whenever we were losing, my Mom would say with determination "PMA—Positive Mental Attitude". She wanted to make sure we had a "we can do this" mindset. This not only worked wonders for our matches but I firmly believe these words—instilled in me as a teenager—stayed with me (consciously or subconsciously) for the quarter century since then. I did not realize it until today in writing this entry but that is how I have lived my life. She raised me into the man I am today . . . always positive and smiling and grateful for so much and going for it in life with a PMA—Positive Mental Attitude. Thanks Mom. You're the best!

⇨ Lesson #207: What's a situation in your life in which you can switch to a Positive Mental Attitude? Note that this lesson is slightly different from Lesson #20, which is to think positively in general.

What did you learn from this week's entries and what changes can you make to live your best life?

_____

_____

_____

_____

12/2—Two days ago, I played football for more than three hours and I am not sore! I have never played organized football so I thought for sure that I would be in some pain today (since it often takes two days for soreness to set in). I feel great though. My key to it was plenty of stretching. Before the game, I did a light jog for a few minutes then stretched for a couple minutes. During the game I stretched often if I had a few spare seconds, and then after the game I stretched for another few minutes.

⇨ Lesson #208: If you are going to do a physical activity that you have not done in a long time or ever, make sure you stretch a lot! This includes not just sports but also things such as shoveling snow or helping someone move. I have heard many people complain of soreness from those activities over the years.

12/3—Serendipity is usually defined as a "happy accident". It's a pretty amazing thing and as you may have noticed, I have had a very serendipitous year! I experienced it two more times yesterday. I arrived at the gym at the same time as this guy Mina. Our arrival was so simultaneous that we almost bumped into each other! Anyway, we had said hello once or twice before but that was it. Yesterday, he asked me "What are you working out today?" I told him back and biceps. He said "Me too. Let's work out together." His body is incredible and his pointers during our workout were excellent. I'm so grateful!

Then last night, I was at Toshi's as usual on Mondays. My friend that I was supposed to meet sent me a text after I got there to say that she could not make it. Ten minutes later, my new friend Tamra Paselk, who I had just met there the week before, walked in and sat down in the open seat at my table! We had SO much fun learning more about each other, enjoying the great music and dancing up a storm. As I have written a couple times already, energy attracts like energy. I love Tamra's energy and I think she would say the same about me. I am so glad we had quality time together for a few hours last night.

⇨ Lesson #209: When you experience serendipity, pause for a moment and enjoy it as one of the awesome things in life. I bet it will make you smile.

12/4—The woman I am working as a Publicist for has sent more work than usual my way lately. It has provided me with some much-needed extra cash as the holidays approach. It does make me a bit of a nerd though right? I am excited about MORE work!

12/5—My November IRA (Individual Retirement Account) statements came today. My investments went up significantly over the last few months. I'm happy that the economy continues to rebound and that the stock market has been on the rise recently. Even though I have no intention of touching these accounts for maybe even a couple decades, it's nice to know they're there in case of emergency. I have other more liquid savings that I can use if necessary in the meantime.

⇨ Lesson #210: Save, save and save! You won't miss the money. I started these accounts when I was 22 or 23 years old. It is amazing to see how much they have grown over the last 20 years. Put a lot of money into your 401(k) at work. If you are self-employed or a freelancer (as is becoming much more common), make sure you are saving money in another way since a 401(k) through a job is not an option.

12/6—Nelson Mandela and my Uncle Augie both passed away overnight last night. I'm sad today. Both were excellent men who lived into their nineties. Here's a quote from Nelson Mandela that is very fitting of the way he (and I) live life: "I am fundamentally an optimist. Whether that comes from nature or nurture, I cannot say. Part of being optimistic is keeping one's head pointed toward the sun, one's feet moving forward. There were many dark moments when my faith in humanity was sorely tested, but I would not and could not give myself up to despair." Well said. The world will miss him.

As for Uncle Augie, God bless him and the healthy, robust life he led. He would have been 91 in two months and was still living on his own and growing tomatoes in his garden out back. I have lots of fond memories of my time with him over the years, especially playing pool in his basement. He always won but I honed my skills. Between his death and Nelson Mandela's, the world lost two great men in their nineties in the last 24 hours.

12/7—This is especially relevant for me given yesterday's post—today, I am grateful for waking up in the morning and being able to get out of bed. This is something that many of us take for granted.

⇨ Lesson #211: If ever you are struggling to express gratitude, waking up can be your first "go to" item. We are fortunate to be living this great thing we call life.

12/8—Today is the penultimate day of my book-writing experience. (I love the word penultimate! I am always excited when I can use what I call an "SAT word"—a great, not very commonly used word that is appropriate for the situation and does not make me sound pretentious as though I'm trying to use a big word to sound smart!) Anyway, on this big day, I'm excited by all the people (including my BFF Anika Johnson) who, as a result of my work for the last year—documenting what I am grateful for every day, and talking about it—are now incredibly grateful for all their blessings. She tells me often she is inspired by me. I have witnessed her changing her mindset these last 12 months and transform herself into someone who focuses on the positives and blessings in life even more than she did before. I hope I hear many such stories of inspiration in the months and years to come. I think there's a movement in society these days, and I am happy to be a part of it.

12/9—Oh my goodness I am done!! I did it! It feels so fantastic having come up with 365 different things to be grateful for. I feel like I still have a lot more. I could go on and on about all the blessings that exist in life and will continue the momentum by posting "Gratitude Extras" on my Russ Terry, Life Coach Facebook page.

I am also grateful that I had the determination to see this part of the project through to completion. I say "this part" because there is still much work to be done to publish the book. Knowing myself as I do though, I won't stop until it's complete and I have the hard copy book in my hands, selling it in person at a book release/book signing party in NYC and at similar parties, workshops and/or speaking engagements here and around the country!

⇨ Lesson #212: See a big project through to completion. The feeling of accomplishment is amazing!

What did you learn from this week's entries and what changes can you make to live your best life?

_____

_____

_____

_____

FUNNY POSTSCRIPT

Remember my loud upstairs neighbors? They have a for sale sign up! I am optimistic they will move out at some point and will be replaced by a quiet new owner. An elderly woman would be lovely!

Do you also recall the loud crossing guard I mentioned? She is back at her post every morning, yelling in her loud voice to all the regulars she sees every day!

These items are perfect examples of the phrase "You win some and you lose some". That's life, and for me, I strive to be grateful for what I win—in other words, the positives—and not worry much about the other stuff.

EPILOGUE

So there it is! When you train your brain to become grateful for things, they just keep coming. I have seen this during my editing process, when I discovered a number of "Gratitude Extras" that are not mentioned in the book. I have been posting these to my business Facebook page and Twitter, so connect with me below if you would like to continue the momentum.

I hope you liked *My Gratitude Journal* and that you're inspired to make some changes in your life—whatever is appropriate for you. I am really proud of the content and also the dedication it took for me to see this book through to completion. I would love to hear your thoughts on it. Feel free to email me (russ@russterrylifecoach.com) and/or connect with me on social media:

www.facebook.com/russell.p.terry

www.facebook.com/russterrylifecoach

www.twitter.com/RTerryLifeCoach

www.linkedin.com/russterrylifecoach

www.instagram.com/russterrylifecoach

Google.com/+russterry

Also, please email me if you want to take part in The Gratitude Project. As I mentioned earlier, you would spend a year documenting what you're grateful for every day. I am planning for my next book to be an anthology from 10-15 different people, each writing a chapter on how focusing on gratitude for 365 straight days has changed their life. I am currently seeking those interested in participating.

.

CPSIA information can be obtained at www.ICGtesting.com
Printed in the USA
BVOW08s1613170314

347872BV00003B/8/P